Crimson Heights

Saundra,
Thank you for God
for Support. May God
Bless you. Peace in The Storm.

2019

Crimson Heights

A WOMAN'S SPIRITUAL PASSAGE THROUGH CELIBACY, INTIMACY, AND SEX

Heather E. Burton, Ph.D.

Crimson Heights:
A Woman's Spiritual Passage through Celibacy Intimacy and Sex

Copyright © 2015 by Heather E. Burton, Ph.D.

ISBN: 978-0-9897526-3-3

Library of Congress Control Number: 2015952902

Published by:

GRIFFIN
SCOTT PRESS
INDIE BESTSELLER PUBLISHING HOUSE

Acknowledgements

So much love to all those who made this project a success. *Crimson Heights* has grown into more than just a book; it's a mission and a ministry. There are so many people to thank for their continued love, pushing, critiques, and compliments.

Mom: I am grateful for your love, guidance, and nurturing, but most importantly for introducing me to Jesus Christ.

Dad: I miss you. You always supported me, and I know that you are still doing so from heaven.

Brother: I appreciate your unconditional love.

Jackie: You've been incredible and far more than a cousin.

G: You are more special than words can describe. Thanks for supporting me and your wonderful, proofreading eye.

The Griffin Scott Press Team: Specifically, my publisher, Regina Griffin. I love you for believing in me and my work. I thank you for your dedication, time, and extra miles.

Misty Schwartz, my publicist: Thank you! You are God-sent.

HEATHER E. BURTON, Ph.D.

I would also like to humbly acknowledge the following people for their gifts and being instrumental in my spiritual and professional growth:

Rev. A. Charles Bowie and the East Mt. Zion Baptist Church family, Rev. Larry W. Howard and the Historic Greater Friendship Church family, Rev. Melvin V. Wade and the Mt. Moriah Church family, Rev. Michael Turner and the Original Harvest Church family, the late Rev. B. W. Noble and all pastors and ministers I've shared affiliation with through work with the National Missionary Baptist Congress, the Center For Community Solutions (especially Sheryl Banks), my friends and family (Demetri, Chandler, the late George R. Head, The Head Family, The Burton Family, The Jones Family, Tré, Kayla, Kimbrella, Tracy, Buffy, Michelle, Portia) and all my sands, specs, and sorors of Delta Sigma Theta Sorority, Inc.

The list of those who have encouraged me extends well beyond the space allotted to give thanks. The overwhelming encouragement has pushed me to complete this project and so much more. Please charge it to my head, not my heart, if I have forgotten to include you in my acknowledgements; know that I am grateful and blessed by your love and heartfelt support.

With much and even more love,
Dr. Heather E. Burton

Foreword

The idea of *Crimson Heights* originated from my own friendship with a group of four girlfriends. Like many women, we would spend our Friday evenings having sister-chats about relationships, marriage, sex, and dating. We openly shared what we wanted in men, what we desired from our relationships, and how we planned to accomplish it. I can still remember the night when one of my sister-friends suggested we put the dialogue from our Friday night talks into a book. I could not have agreed more. Hence, the story of *Crimson Heights* was born.

Initially, the book was intended to chronicle the lives of four adult friends and how they survived the trials of dating, marriage, and intimate relationships with the opposite sex. But as I began to write, the story started to manifest its own direction. I felt like God was taking me on a different course. My manuscript began to focus more on how women and teen girls dealt with issues around sex. In retrospect, I believe my line of work at the time had a profound effect on the story's ultimate narrative.

Midway through writing the book, I began a project at work that focused on improving suburban school curriculums in Northeast Ohio. The curriculum specifically covered two courses: Abstinence Only until Marriage and Comprehensive Abstinence-Based Sex Education. My work helped me gain a better understanding of the pressures and decisions young girls deal with surrounding sex. I began to study the alarming statistics of pregnancy rates and sexually transmitted diseases.

In 2005, East Cleveland, Ohio, revealed reports of this rise of ten and eleven-year-old girls who were becoming pregnant. A 2002–2003 report by the City of Cleveland Department of Public Health and the Ohio Department of Health cited that STDs (including gonorrhea and chlamydia) had been on the rise since 1997. In 2003, Cleveland chlamydia rates rose to 1,161.4 per 100,000 (1 in every 86) residents, a 10.6 percent increase from 2002. STD infections among teens (ages 15–19) reached significant levels with 6,973 per 100,000 (1 in every 14) infected with chlamydia, a 4.3 percent increase over 2002. Gonorrhea infections were 3,696 per 100,000 (1 in every 27), a 6.5 percent decrease from 2002.

At the time of testing, 8.6 percent of teens between the ages of 15–19 were positive for both chlamydia and gonorrhea. And more saddening than any of the statistical data uncovered was that the fastest growing number of HIV/AIDS cases were African-American females. What were these girls seeking? Did they really enjoy sex that much, or were they engaging in sex for other reasons?

As God intervened and changed the story's message, I realized I needed to address and speak candidly about the issues that exist between females, sex, and sexuality. So the purpose of this book evolved into a movement to get women and young girls to understand that their decisions about sex can carry a lifetime effect. In pursuit, I concentrated on making *Crimson Heights*, its characters, and their storylines, as realistic as possible. I endeavored to write a story that would touch and resonate with the masses.

In that quest, some of the content that I consider to be PG-13 may be viewed as explicit by others. However, I did not write *Crimson* with any intent to add gratuitous shock value. My only hope was to deliver a message that was real, believable, and would give readers a true sense of how life and irresponsible sex can be a toxic collision course.

To my Christian brothers and sisters who find this book risqué or even superfluous, I pose this question: Could a young woman in your life be a carbon copy of Meghan? The 15-year-old daughter of Sister Jones, Meghan sings in the choir, and prominently serves on the junior usher board. She's a young girl who welcomes visitors on Youth Sunday in her white ruffled blouse and A-line skirt down to her ankles, but to the surprise of many, is not a virgin. If there's a Meghan in your life, you should understand why this book is mission critical in our Christian talk and Christian walk.

Meghan's character may not personify a young girl in your life, but it may be the daughter, niece, or granddaughter of someone you know. As a Christian community, it is our responsibility to be our brother's keeper. Thus, if only one reader decides to opt for celibacy until marriage, or decides unprotected sex is something he or she is not willing to risk and starts to use protection to prevent catching a disease or creating an unwanted pregnancy, then my writing has not been in vain.

Contents

CHAPTER I

Kennedy & Reagan

*E*ach stride flaunted the striation of Kennedy's strong calves and muscular thighs. Wearing black with white side-striped jogging pants, a matching sports bra and Adidas running shoes, Kennedy was right in the middle of her workout when her cell phone rang. *I'm not answering that,* she thought. Increasingly annoyed by the sound of her ringing phone, she amped the treadmill speed to 7.5 miles per hour and began to run faster. After the third ring, she grabbed her iPhone, almost simultaneously dropping it and losing her balance.

"Ewwwh," she groaned, breathing heavily, before finally gasping enough breath to utter, "Hello."

"Kennedy?" Reagan shrieked in an interrogating tone from the other end.

"Yes!" Kennedy snapped, continuing to run on the treadmill.

"Why are you breathing like a serial killer?" Reagan probed.

"What, Reagan? I'm working out!"

"Working out or getting a piece?" Kennedy could sense the smirk on Reagan's face by the chuckle in her voice.

The seemingly random phone call annoyed the hell out of Kennedy. Everyone, especially Reagan, knew how seriously she took her workouts.

Reagan calling her to joke around in the middle of her routine was a pain in the you-know-what.

Aggravated, Kennedy replied, "I told you! I'm at the gym. Working out! Where you should be."

"Oh, so you got jokes, huh?" Reagan sarcastically rebutted.

"I'm not joking, Reagan. Have you not noticed how much weight you've gained?"

One o'clock was usually a quiet time at the gym, basically a starting lineup of the status quo cast members. The old man who walked the treadmill at two miles per hour. The annoyingly friendly older woman who talked to any and everybody that would stop and listen. Those who did absolutely nothing and only came to the gym to socialize and run game. The highlight was the chick that every man who walked into a gym hoped to stumble across. The one who wouldn't be caught dead lifting a one-pound weight, unless a man was lying under it. Never to be upstaged, though, was the brutha rockin' the tight spandex shorts with his shirt tied in front, right above his belly button. And certainly not the least of them—the personal training staff! They completed the midday ensemble, walking about sporting uniforms so tight they could easily be mistaken for the hand-me-downs of their elementary-school-aged sibling. Outfits that typically consisted of a pair of shorts, complemented by an infant-sized muscle shirt, respectively displaying their bird chests and underdeveloped parrot legs.

Sometimes the whole gym scene reminded Kennedy of Friday nights at the club, featuring the sweaty-stalker guy, spewing a barrage of one-liners that rolled off his tongue like bullets, "Hey, Red! Yo, baby, what's your name? Yo, yo! Redbone? You looking sexy as a mutha! What's up, thickness?"

Justin was one guy at the gym who was an exception to the visual melee. He was six-two with a body for the gods. He had competed in a ton of weightlifting competitions, and from the looks of his body, he had won more than his share. Back in the day, Kennedy had a piece of Justin, briefly. She flew the coop when she realized she couldn't put up with a man who thought he was prettier. He could never resist the temptation of blowing himself a kiss anytime he saw his reflection. No woman could deal with that kind of crap, especially not Kennedy.

Every weekday afternoon, one could count on a Kennedy Johnson sighting at Fitness World Gym. Over the years she had worked hard to stay in shape, and seeing that most men recognized the *assets* of her efforts, not a second of her commitment seemed to be wasted. In fact, there weren't too many men who didn't find Kennedy to be a modern-day brick house. At five-nine, one hundred sixty pounds, with curves in all the right places, Kennedy knew how to work what her momma had given her.

She maintained a four- to five-day weekly workout regimen, complete with forty-five minutes of cardio and thirty minutes of strength training. The intensity of her workouts kept her in the gym for no less than two hours each visit.

Anxious to get off the phone and back to her workout she barked, "What's up, Reagan? What could be so important?"

"I need your help." This time Reagan sounded restless.

"With what?" Kennedy shouted back in aggravation.

"Lexi's party!"

If Kennedy could have wrapped her hands around Reagan's neck at that moment, she would have strangled her. "Reagan, I know you didn't call me to talk about a party that's easily a whole three months away."

"Yeah, I did, Kennedy. Anyway, at three o'clock in the afternoon, most people are still at work."

"Well, some people have flex schedules. So, thank you very much, motor mouth! Don't you have an embezzler or some criminal you need to be somewhere defending?" Kennedy dug at Reagan in a cynical tone.

"Nope, I put most of them behind bars before noon. So, I'm free to focus all my attention on annoying you."

It suddenly hit Kennedy that Reagan was not going to let her off the phone until she got what she was calling for. "Lucky me. Come on, Reagan. What do you really want?"

"I told you! Lexi's thirtieth birthday is coming up, and it has to be a grand celebration."

"Lexi's turning thirty? Wow, I can't believe it. It seems like only yesterday we were playing hopscotch and jacks. Reagan, I know you remember jacks."

"Honey, who doesn't? Not that fond of a memory for me, considering that jacks were a good twenty years before my boobs dropped, toosh spread, and abs morphed into the shape of a washing machine instead of my ideal washboard."

"You're only thirty-five, Reagan."

"Kennedy, I'm thirty-five with a fat butt."

"If your fat butt is bothering you that much, go to the gym!"

"Girl, I don't have time for the gym. I like the shortcuts—diets, pills, and formulas."

"What do you mean, you don't have time? You have time right now, while you're calling me, disturbing my groove."

"Kennedy, seriously, I don't have the patience for the gym. By the time I drive there, work out, and drive home, two hours would have vanished. People are killing themselves with these crazy workout schedules, trying to look like the chiseled bodies and skinny people they see in magazines and on television. Why not just take the time to eat right or eat less?"

Kennedy laughed uncontrollably. "Whatever! What has eating right done for you—other than added thirty pounds to your already fat butt?"

"Okay, that's fair. Lately, I have added a tad of volume to my backside."

Kennedy was determined to finish her workout without further interruption. "Okay then, voluminous backside, let me call you when I'm done. Give me another hour or so."

Before her weight gain, Reagan used to be Ms. It. She was as fine as a bottle of imported wine. Age had caught up with her, and her metabolism had taken a dive into the deep end. Her womanly figure had blossomed into a size sixteen, much larger than the familiar size six she had touted like a trophy.

She was obsessed with shedding the weight and had tried everything to get it off. One week, she would detox with a shot of vinegar every morning. The next, she'd follow a strict regimen of vitamins chased with a shot of some type of metabolic booster. She had tried every diet known to modern man, but she still found herself in an endless cycle of lose, gain, lose—gain, with double-digit interest.

She loved food and it loved her back passionately. She was the type who could suck down a super-sized, high-fat meal every couple of hours. McDonald's. Burger King. Taco Bell. If it came in a bag or wrapped in waxed paper, Reagan would devour it. But she was honest about her struggle, and openly admitted she was a woman who cursed exercise and clung to food.

In all her struggles, she somehow managed to be cool and confident with her thickness. Carrying extra weight to her was like a full head of weave to a bald woman. She used it to her advantage! A successful lawyer, whether a size sixteen or six, she could work any courtroom. Not to mention her ultimate ego booster—a husband who worshipped her and made her feel like she was still Ms. It, or rather, Mrs. It.

Reagan and Ryan had been married for five years, and every day he admired her more—sometimes ad nauseam. Ryan was hardworking, a production supervisor for a manufacturing company, and the complete nonchalant opposite of Reagan. He was comfortable sitting back, patiently watching, and hardly ever becoming hostile or angry, which explained why they got along so well. Reagan would rant and rave about the smallest things. Listening to her, one would never think Ryan had a romantic bone in his body. Quite the contrary.

Once, he hired a limo to pick up Reagan and take her to the spa for a day of pampering. Afterwards, he met her there with a new outfit that he had picked out all by himself and took Reagan out for a night of dinner and dancing.

"Just because I love you and think you're great," he told her. Nothing like a man who adores his woman. At her fattest or skinniest, Ryan always saw Reagan as perfect in every light.

Reagan Rand was Crimson Heights' board chairperson, lawyer, legal advisor, and consultant. Crimson was a local performing arts center. Reagan, Kennedy, Alexis, and Amber had worked there together for years. Work, the place where many women meet and befriend the women closest to them. The type of friendships where one woman plays the pseudo role of mother—telling the others what to do, how to do it, when to do it, and whether it's right or wrong. Reagan took on that protective parental role in the group of women, and she always gave her advice...welcomed or not. Albeit, she was fair and consistent with her firmness. You could always depend on her to back you up if you were right, but she never minced words if she thought you were wrong.

As executive director, Kennedy spent the greater part of every week working at least sixty hours to keep Crimson afloat. Kennedy and Reagan had been friends for almost seven years. Both were former bank employees and used to working around a bunch of blue suits that functioned like they had sticks shoved up their behinds. A mutual sorority sister had introduced them, and with Kennedy in charge of marketing and Reagan being Summit Savings and Trust's legal counselor, they became fast friends.

But with each passing day, Kennedy had grown to hate her job at Summit more and more. Her loathing ultimately led her to submit her letter of resignation. She had no idea how she would continue to support herself, but in her frustration she felt nothing else could be much worse.

The day of her resignation, Kennedy explained to her supervisor, "Mrs. Jones, I believe I have reached my maximum potential here. I think it's time for me to venture into other career opportunities." Before Kennedy could start her next sentence, Mrs. Jones had managed to piss her off.

Mockingly, "Well, Kennedy, I too believe you have reached your maximum potential here at Summit Savings and Trust, but as a marketing specialist, I can't imagine there would be that many other opportunities for you to explore." What she really wanted to say was, *I can't stand the ground you walk on because you're smarter than me, dress better, and look better.*

When Kennedy began her tenure at Summit, she knew it would be a short one from the first time she caught Mrs. Jones rolling her inspecting eyes at her in contempt. Every morning, Mrs. Jones had a faithful ritual of checking Kennedy out from the crown of her head to the soles of her shoes, eyeballing every detail about her.

"Oh, that's a lovely necklace you're wearing today, Ms. Johnson."

"Why thank you very much, Mrs. Jones." The cattiness had irritated Kennedy…almost as much as having her workouts disturbed.

Reagan, on the other hand, held a special place in her heart for Summit. Kennedy never understood why. Reagan attended undergraduate school at Spelman College in Atlanta, Georgia, and law school at Case Western Reserve University in Cleveland, Ohio. She loved giving people instruction, which was probably why she and Mrs. Jones *didn't* butt heads. In the back of her mind, Mrs. Jones understood that if pushed, Reagan wouldn't hesitate to conjure a lawsuit scheme that would get her fired before she could brew her morning cup of Folgers. In fact, when Mrs. Jones would see Reagan walking down the same side of the bank hallway, she would shiver and cross to the other side. Eight years into her career at Summit Savings and Trust, Reagan was promoted to the director of law and personal attorney for a lot of the same blue-suit-wearing banking tight-asses that she once worked for.

Kennedy decided that being confined to a desk all day just wasn't for her. She had majored in theater at The Ohio State University and embellished her job application to get the position at Summit. Something about 'possessing some outreach marketing and writing skills…blah, blah, blah' happened to be the perfect catch phrase to land her the gig. Her natural abilities as a marketer had contributed to her success, but she also enjoyed working as an advocate to ensure that culture and arts were focal points in the lives of young people.

After finally chasing Reagan off the phone, Kennedy only had cardio and abs left to complete. "Excuse me," a man's voice uttered so close she was startled off her treadmill.

"Yes?" she asked, slowly turning to see the face behind the velvety voice. The specimen she saw made her mouth drop, and spit pooled in the corners. She found herself gazing at what had to be the finest man in all of America as a six-foot-four Adonis stood before her. He was Hershey's chocolate brown—like a three-layered decadent cake topped with whipped chocolate icing. Muscles protruded from every section of his body, straight through his clothes. *Okay, Kennedy*, she thought to herself, *close your mouth. Close your mouth, girl!*

His teeth gleamed as he asked, "Are you almost finished with the treadmill?"

There was something about his eyes. They were hypnotic, even sensual. As they locked with hers, Kennedy felt a warm sensation jolt through her body. The voice in her head warned her: *Your heart is about to stop beating. Your lungs are no longer getting air, and your limbs are going numb. Breathe. Breathe, dammit!* Just the sight of him made Kennedy's body rumble with sensation.

It took her nearly a full minute before a sound emerged from her mouth. "I'm almost done, just two minutes of cool-down left." If treadmills were made for two, Kennedy would have invited him for a couple's run.

"Okay, just let me know when you're finished. I'll be over in the corner stretching," the response from his deep voice echoed in her ears.

"Sure." She smiled.

As she watched him walk away, her mind shifted into a daydream snatched right out of a Tyler Perry movie. Crimson and cream candles symmetrically lined a church altar while the sunlight's reflection beamed through stained-glass windows. Colorful lilies and simple carnations accented with baby's breath flooded the church foyer. Her mother was nestled prominently on the first row, weeping tears of joy, and Kennedy's grandparents were seated nearby, adding more delight to the atmosphere. The coco-chocolate man from the gym was dressed in a black tux, positioned front and center at the altar. His broad shoulders and muscles perfectly contoured every seam of his jacket. His hair was freshly cut; his beard and mustache highlighted the richness of his skin. As music began to play, Kennedy and her father entered the church, walking arm in arm to the sweet sounds of "Love" by Kirk Franklin.

Thump, thump, thump ... *bam!* ... was the sound of Kennedy hitting her knee on the treadmill railing and flying into the air. By the time she had snatched out the treadmill's safety cord and it stopped, she found herself lying flat on her back in the middle of a crowded gym. How completely humiliating.

Kennedy was looking to add some spice to her life but not the kind that had her lying on her back in the gym. Adult recreation was a must for Kennedy, so there was always time for fun, but her social résumé read like a scripted version of *The Young and the Restless* soap opera. Not married. Not going steady. Not committed. And like most thirty-two-year-old females, not truly ready to settle down. In her dreams, she would have already been married by twenty-five, had a couple of kids by twenty-eight, and forged a solid career by thirty. Instead, by the time she had hit twenty-five, she was kicking it at the club Thursday through Saturday.

The men in her life were mere entertainment packages. She would bore of them rather quickly, and they would come and go. There was Reggie, David, Escobar, John, Dontae, Paul, Kevin, George, Roger ... the list went on for miles. Every week, she would have a scheduled dinner at seven, hit the club by eleven, and be in bed by two. The days that followed felt like a replay of *Groundhog Day*.

She was completing a master's degree and didn't have time for a husband, child, or anything more serious. It was all about Kennedy; what she wanted, what she needed, and what she hoped to accomplish. She just didn't see room in her life for a serious commitment, but now, at thirty-two, her uterus was nearing its expiration date. In her head, she could hear the tick-tock sound of the time running out on her biological clock. All explanation for why she would sometimes get a little carried away when she saw a man that caught her interest.

"Excuse me, I'm finished with the treadmill. It's all yours," she said bashfully with a crooked grin.

"Thank you." He grinned back.

"You're more than welcome." *Say something else, Kennedy! Say something!* "How long do you ride on that thing?" Then she thought to herself, *No! That was dumb! Couldn't you have come up with something less juvenile?*

Just as the thought raced through her head, he answered, "About 30 minutes."

Think of another question, Kennedy! He's not biting, she thought frantically, but only came up with, "Do you work out often?"

"No," he replied without looking up. He didn't even pause to make eye contact or confirm if the conversation had ended. Instead, he hopped on the treadmill, pressed the start button, and began running without saying another word.

"Have a good workout," she said flirtatiously, hoping he would be watching her strut away.

Kennedy could not believe she was flirting at the gym; it was something she vowed to never do. She hated the idea of the gym being a meat market. It was a place for health-conscious productivity, and now she was tainting her haven by flirting with this fine mystery man. Truth of the matter, she had not seen a man that caliber of fine in a while. If she didn't seize the moment, God only knew when another opportunity would come again.

Still, she had walked away, being paid hardly any attention and having little conversation. She paused mentally to methodically weigh her recovery options. She could shower, dress, apply a full face of makeup, and prance back onto the workout floor or even loiter in the lobby where she could easily be seen. Her second and most sensible option was to snap back to reality and rely on fate to place them in the same room again. She decided to put her second option into play.

"See you, Kennedy. Have a good day!" Lisa said, waving bye to Kennedy.

Lisa worked the reception desk at the gym. "Hey, Lisa, did you see a dark-skinned guy pass by, about six-four?"

"Nope," she answered bluntly.

"Don't you sign in everybody?" Kennedy question anxiously.

"Yeah, but I must've been in the restroom when he came in. I do have to pee sometimes, you know. Why are you asking anyway, Ms. Don't Bother Me When I'm at the Gym?"

"Where did you get the impression that I don't want to be bothered at the gym?" Kennedy asked, embarrassed. It was unquestionably true, but she never realized that others could pick up on her vibe.

"Kennedy, everybody knows that about you. It's clear that you want to be left alone when you work out."

"Is it that obvious?" Kennedy asked, concerned that people could have the wrong read on her. Though she hated being interrupted during her workouts, she felt she was pleasant for the most part.

"You've been coming here for years, so I think anybody would have caught the drift by now. You're heart-attack serious about your workouts, Kennedy! It's no biggie. Trust me, you're not the only one."

"Wow, I didn't know people could sense that about me."

"No flirting or anything. It's all about getting it in," Lisa said, staring down the impeccable muscle tone of Kennedy's physique. "But look at your body! You can tell you work out religiously."

"Which is a result of not allowing anything to distract me when I'm here," Kennedy boasted.

"Back to your question though, what about this guy?" Lisa pounded with a curiosity that was borderline nosey. She wondered why Kennedy was asking about a man.

Kennedy had to be quick on her feet and think of a good reason for asking. *Come on, spit it out! What would be a good excuse? Why am I asking about this man? Why?* "Well, I thought I recognized him from a work convention, and I wanted to invite him to speak to my girls at Crimson. Since you check everybody in, I figured you would know who he was. Now that I know you didn't see him come in, it's a moot issue. Maybe I'll run into him another time. Anyway, gotta go."

"Just go back to the workout floor and ask him," Lisa encouraged.

"I can't. I have a meeting to go to," Kennedy claimed, dashing out the front door of the gym.

She was lying through her teeth, but she wanted to leave before she was caught in another one. Nonetheless, it didn't keep her from wondering if she had forfeited her only chance to exchange contact information with the man of mythical proportions of fineness. Could he have been her knight in shining armor? He could have been the missing king to remedy her queen of lonely hearts. Had she walked away from the man who could have been the one to love her for all of eternity?

A double dose of reality kicked in and she convinced herself that she had made the best decision in taking her chances on running into him again. Kennedy's ultimate belief was that whatever was meant to be would eventually be. It was pointless to keep pondering the matter. She lived by strict rules where dating was concerned, and her first commandment was that a woman never chased a man. Her thought process was if a man found a woman interesting enough, he would find the time to pursue her. If he didn't, and the woman held to a standard of not being the chaser, either outcome would only benefit her dignity. In all her mental gymnastics and justifying, the truth was still that Kennedy felt she probably would never see him again.

CHAPTER 2

The Two A's

Besides Reagan, Amber and Alexis were two of Kennedy's closest friends. Amber was the voice instructor and taught private lessons twice a week in the evening at Crimson. Alexis taught dance: jazz, tap, and group ballet classes. Over the years, Crimson's enrollment had tripled, justifying the center's need to be open twelve hours a day, six days a week. As a strong observer of the Sabbath, no classes were scheduled on Sundays.

Grandma Annie Mae had instilled in Kennedy "Sunday is the Lord's day," and she'd held onto the wisdom of her nana's teachings. It was also the reason she refused to go clubbing on Saturdays. She found it hypocritical to do her secular dance floor hand wave on Saturday nights, then follow it with a worship and praise wave on Sunday mornings. Sitting in service with a hangover, barely able to stay awake, and smelling like a brewery was no longer her thang. Kennedy now limited her socializing to Friday evenings, and that was mainly for networking. But, of course, with networking there were always those well-deserved glasses of wine. She figured Jesus had turned water into wine, so why not enjoy it? In many ways, she still had a lot of maturing to do.

Tuesdays and Thursdays were busy evenings at Crimson, which meant twelve-hour days for Kennedy. She would arrive at the office by 9:00 a.m., leave for a couple of hours around lunchtime and come back at 3:00 p.m. to prepare for evening classes. The other days were mainly handled by her staff, unless someone called off. Kennedy loved the fact that Amber and Alexis were rarely absent without notice. She always wondered if their dutifulness was a byproduct of their solid friendship with her, or if they just authentically loved their jobs.

The day had started as one where Kennedy felt the need for me-time, pushing the return of her afternoon break to 4:30 p.m. rather than the usual. She checked her voice mail, and the first message was from Reagan.

"Hey, Kennedy, I know we talked yesterday about Lexi's party. You said you would call me back, but you never did. Wanted to know if Lexi is working today. Call me!" Reagan sounded desperate.

Kennedy slowly pecked Reagan's number on her phone's keypad, dreading the conversation and wondering what she wanted. Probably nothing, but Kennedy took some relief in at least knowing that Reagan wasn't interrupting another one of her workouts.

"Hello."

"Hey, Reagan, what's up?" Kennedy probed.

"Nothing much. Just checking on Lexi."

Kennedy thought to herself, *then why the hell didn't you call Lexi?* But since Reagan genuinely sounded concerned, Kennedy decided to be nice and asked, "Why are you checking on Lexi?"

"Wanted to see if she was at work today."

"Yeah, she came in around four. Why'd you wanna know?" Kennedy sensed that Reagan was withholding information. As if she knew something was wrong with Lexi but wasn't telling her.

"I got a message from her earlier. She said she was feeling really tired today and didn't know whether she would make it in. So, I was just checking to see if she showed." Kennedy could hear the stress in Reagan's voice, but it was also classic Reagan. She was a worrywart who had a tendency to always be concerned about something or someone. "I'm worried, Kennedy. It could be serious."

"Reagan, just chill. If it was that serious, Lexi would have called in." Realizing Reagan was being her typical hyper-anxious self, eased Kennedy's mind. "Well, she's here, mama. Is that all you wanted? I was about to start panicking, too. You sounded like someone had died or something. Anyway, I have to run, but I'll check on her in a few minutes when I catch up on my work."

Kennedy's head was spinning in circles trying to figure out where to begin attacking her workload for the day. There were a few urgent matters she needed to handle regarding impending shipments for Crimson. The teachers and students were preparing for a recital, and the kids still needed several items for their dance classes. She gave the task priority over following up with Lexi.

"Hi, this is Kennedy Johnson from Crimson Heights Performing Arts Center. I'm checking on a shipment originally scheduled to arrive yesterday, but it's still missing."

Alexis, affectionately referred to as Lexi, was the youngest of the Crimson ladies. She was turning thirty on April 5, and Reagan was in anal overload mode about the details of her birthday party. Each was guilty of babying Lexi, partly because she'd lost her mother to cancer right after graduating from college. Kennedy believed it was one of the reasons Lexi had prematurely married at twenty-two. The loss of her mother was crushing, and Lexi missed her support. They were close as twin sisters. Their kindredness reminded Kennedy a lot of her relationship with her own mom. Only Kennedy and her mom had not developed their closeness until Kennedy's late twenties. Something unexplainable happened when Kennedy reached that age, and they became the best of friends. Kennedy talked as openly to her mom as she did her best buds, though within reason. She never forgot the fact it was still her mom. Unlike them, Lexi and her mom had an unbreakable bond from the moment Lexi popped into the world. Lexi idolized her mother in many ways, and focused more on a relationship with her than God. Maybe the sayings of the old saints bore some truth, "If you let something get in the place of God, he'll move it out of the way." Had God taken Lexi's mom to shift her focus to him?

For every occurrence in life, the old saints always had an explanation backed by scripture.

Shortly after the death of her mother, Lexi married Ray. He was her college sweetheart, and she adored him like a rat loves cheese. Ray was a nerdy guy who knew how to camouflage his geek factor. He majored in economics, received his master's from Rutgers, and landed a job crunching numbers for some big firm. No one truly had the slightest idea of what he really did, but he was good to Lexi, and that alone seemed to diffuse inquiring minds.

It wasn't a shock when Ray married Lexi; everyone knew he eventually would. The only surprise was it happened so soon after college. They traveled a lot in the beginning of their marriage; a big factor in why five years passed before their first son was born. Tré had grown into a rambunctious three-year-old, and Lexi happily spent the majority of her time nurturing him.

Even being the youngest and having the least life experiences, Alexis was Kennedy's spiritual inspiration. Alexis lived, breathed, and flaunted being a church girl. Being reared in church doesn't always determine how a person turns out, but it was a blueprint for Alexis. Her late mother ran a tight ship and always threatened, "If you live in my house, you're going to church." Her mom had set up a virtual billboard in her head, constantly advertising that her choice in a husband needed to be a God-fearing one. Ray fit the bill.

Lexi didn't waste time in finding out how he measured on her mother's yardstick. She drilled him on their first date, "Are you saved? Have you accepted Jesus Christ as your personal Savior?" Whenever Lexi referenced the story of their first encounter, Kennedy was always awestruck by Lexi's boldness to table the important discussion of religion right off the top.

Lexi's outlook was if you couldn't ask a man about the convictions of his spirit, he probably was one you shouldn't be interested in getting to know. She was really knowledgeable and a faithful student of the Bible. She used the word of God to keep everyone's moral barometer in check, especially Kennedy's.

Determining Ray's seriousness about his salvation spoke volumes about what Lexi valued in a relationship. She didn't revere money, material things, or even sex. Her respect and standards rested on the God her man served and his degree of faithfulness. Kennedy only hoped she could reach Lexi's level of spiritual awakening, and relinquish her fears of running a man off with overt discussions of religion.

Kennedy wasn't as grounded, but she knew stable Christian friends could benefit each other's spiritual growth. She prayed that Lexi's iron spirit would continue to sharpen hers. She longed for the day when God would bless her with a husband who would make worshipping and attending church a priority. She wanted to hear the man she loved utter the words, "Babe, let's get ready for church." Instead of hearing the all too familiar pushback, "Church? Naw, baby. You know Sunday is game day. I can't go to church!" She had never met a man who was smart enough to figure out he could tape the game and watch if after church.

Kennedy believed if a man didn't have a spiritual foundation, there was nothing to guide his inner battle between right and wrong or good and evil. She saw women as creatures that could easily commit to any man they loved, but on the other hand, she viewed men as ones who needed a little extra *umph* to play the commitment card. Men, just being accountable to their wives or significant others, didn't seem stringent enough. They needed someone or something more, something higher: Jesus, Allah, Buddha, Jehovah. A force with bigger omnipresent eyes, more powerful than a woman, and void of penis-guiding influences. Not that a penis was a problem, but it certainly had the potential to create issues when used in the place of a brain.

Frustrated over being on hold for almost ten minutes, Kennedy was about to hang up when she heard a man's voice bellow, "Hello, Ms. Johnson? Yes, I was able to locate your package. The shipment should arrive tomorrow. If you don't receive it, please let us know."

"Thanks for your help, sir, and I hope we do receive it tomorrow." Kennedy had mastered the protocol of remaining professional to get the outcome she wanted in business settings. A hot head usually led to an argument and ended with nothing being accomplished. She knew a kinder, more amenable approach meant future discounted rates and free stuff for her troubles.

Just as she hung up the phone, there was a knock on her office door.

"*Qué pasa*, Kennedy?"

"Hey, Amber. What's up?"

"The usual."

For Amber, the usual meant she had another Hell Date story to share. Amber had a scheduled date every other night with a different guy. She was a lunatic where dating was concerned, and went through men with the speed of checking out at a ten-items-or-less grocery lane—*pretty quickly*. Her downfall was her ever elusive quest for a man to take care of her financially. Wouldn't say she was a gold digger, but she wasn't checking for no broke … ummm.

Let's just say, she didn't get the memo about men not wanting to be perpetually responsible for women who weren't their wives! She failed to realize few men found reward in putting their hard-earned money toward a random woman's upkeep. Some didn't mind helping her out, but most were turned off because she'd move in for the kill in the first thirty days. She wore her motives around her neck like a bowtie, so the majority of her suitors only stuck around for a couple of dates.

Growing up, Amber wanted for nothing. She, too, had an influential grandmother, just of a different kind. Her granny would caution her, "If a man can't pay your bills, he ain't worth the paper a dollar bill is printed on." And that's exactly what Amber went through life believing. She thought a man's express purpose for being on earth was to take care of a woman, namely her.

"You went out last night?" Kennedy asked before realizing she was jumping into the lion's den. She really didn't desire to hear all the grisly details of Amber's dating life, even though she was going to hear it whether she wanted or not.

Seemingly agitated, Amber answered, "Yeah, I went out with Greg. The guy I met at the grocery store."

"How was it?"

CRIMSON HEIGHTS

Rolling her eyes, she couldn't mask the disgust on her face.
"He's cheap!"

Knowing Amber couldn't stand a cheap man, Kennedy played devil's
advocate and further instigated, "And what's wrong with that?"

Smirking, Amber smacked her lips. "Frugal is one thing, but cheap is
uncalled for, especially on the first date! Kennedy, you know good and
gosh darn well you wouldn't give a man a second date if he was cheap
on the first one." Kennedy could always get a rise out of Amber on the
topic of a man spending his money.

Oddly enough, they both agreed a man should never pinch pennies
where dating was concerned, and being a spendthrift on a first date was
a deal breaker! The only difference was Amber expected a man to wine
and dine her as if it were his God-appointed duty, while Kennedy simply
appreciated it. It was a conversation they often split hairs on, particularly when Amber met someone she felt didn't splurge to her standard.

"Amber, you can't control how a man spends his money." Kennedy
only entertained the banter to aggravate her. "I don't see anything wrong
with being frugal. Anyway, there's a big difference in being frugal and
plain ol' cheap."

Placing her hands on the little bit of hips she had, Amber scorned,
"Come on, Kennedy! A man who's frugal is cheap. Ain't no difference!"

Reluctantly, Kennedy shook her head. "Not true. Frugal people are
conscientious about their spending, which is not necessarily cheap."

Frustrated, Amber began to leave Kennedy's office as she turned and
said, "Cheap, frugal, whatever—it's all a sign of him spending less on me!"

Kennedy burst into laughter knowing none of Amber's whining meant
a hill of beans, because it still wouldn't be a challenge for Greg to get
another date out of her. And sure enough, Amber confirmed they'd
already made plans to see each other that very night. Amber never gave
up hope that the second time around could be her gold-digging charm.

Kennedy had a hard time keeping track of Amber's dates. Amber
was independent and in a position to take care of herself. She certainly
didn't need a man for that, but she enjoyed a man's company...and sex.

19

"Anyway, Amber, I thought you tutored Reign last night," Kennedy questioned, shuffling through the pile of papers on her desk, trying to locate invoices for impending shipments.

Amber occasionally tutored a few of Crimson's students in math. Lately, one of them, Reign, had become preoccupied with something. The previous night, Reign called Amber to cancel her tutoring session. Kennedy, too, was becoming increasingly worried by Reign's change in behavior.

"Reign has been acting sort of strange lately."

Stopping just short of the doorway of Kennedy's office, Amber paused and addressed her, "Strange how?"

"I don't know." Kennedy couldn't quite put her finger on it, but she knew something was different with Reign's behavior.

"It's probably nothing. Maybe she's just going through puppy love heartbreak." Amber laughed. "That or being pissed on by a dog."

"Girl, you are a nut! I worry about you. Let me go check on Lexi. Reagan called and said she wasn't feeling well today." Kennedy moved from behind her desk and began walking toward her office door.

"I saw her earlier. She looked tired and said she was going to the studio to lie down before class. I told her to call me if she needed me to sub for her," Amber shared.

"I'll go down and see what's going on." Kennedy dashed through the corridor and down two flights of stairs to Crimson's basement.

As she approached the dance studio, she saw Lexi sitting in a corner. Standing about five-foot-four, Lexi had the body of a Greek goddess. It was a frame that was gifted to her by nature, and being a dancer since the age of three, her natural metabolism was enough to maintain the vessel. She had light caramel-colored skin and was very meticulous about the care and styling of her hair. She maintained a weekly ritual of getting her hair done, nails manicured, and face professionally primped.

She was surprisingly conservative for her age. You would never catch her in anything revealing or even sexy, but she had a walk that drove men to drink. It just naturally made her sensual, even though she never tried. She was a chick who could capture the attention of any man, *or woman*, for that matter. We playfully called her Sexy Lexi. She had danced all around the world, from Europe to Broadway, where she'd met Amber. They were both performing in the Broadway rendition of *The Wiz*.

Kennedy peeped her head into the dance studio. "Hey, Lexi, you all right?" Lexi was pale; her bronzed complexion resembled porcelain more than anything.

"I'm okay, Kennedy." Lexi's voice was weak and shaky.

"Apparently, Reagan doesn't think so. She called and said you mentioned you were feeling kind of tired today."

"No, really, I'm fine."

"You don't look fine," Kennedy rebutted, clearly seeing that something was wrong.

"Well, I am." Lexi managed to get the words out just before crouching over to hold her stomach.

"Do you want me to find a substitute for your class? Have you eaten anything?"

"No, I haven't felt like eating." Still holding her stomach, Lexi could feel her intestines twisting in a knot. It was a pain that felt like someone had placed a vice grip on her stomach and turned it every time she breathed. But she kept her composure, not wanting Kennedy to know how much pain she was in. It was a pain she had felt on and off for the last few days, so she knew it would pass. Maybe it was just a stomach flu or some bug she had caught from one of the students.

"Could it have been something you ate yesterday then?" Kennedy probed.

"Maybe. Ray and I took Tré to this new kid's restaurant. I had nachos, so it could be that."

"Can I get you anything?"

"No, Kennedy. I was feeling a little exhausted earlier. I haven't been able to keep anything down, so the lack of food is probably what has me so weak. I'll let one of my students lead most of today's class."

"I can ask Amber to excuse Kayla."

Kayla was one of Crimson's best dance students. She had competed nationally in dozens of competitions and always brought home the gold.

She leapt at any chance to be in dance class. She lived to dance, and would be willing to help Lexi out.

"Oh my God, Kayla would love that, Kennedy. You know how she feels about Amber's voice class."

"They complain, but they love her to death."

"I know. Hopefully Amber doesn't have anything too vigorous planned."

Amber was a little rough when it came to voice class. She believed children and adults could only reach their maximum potential with strict discipline. Her classes ran like an army boot camp. She was overwhelmingly proud of her Latino roots (her father was Hispanic and her mother black) and it reflected in her classes. She mixed songs in Spanish and English in a manner that highlighted the diversity Crimson was known for. Amber was an excellent instructor who knew music and could teach anyone.

The majority of the parents and children loved her. The only complaint against her had been the time when Amber told a Crimson parent, Ms. Curry, that the bad apple didn't fall too far from the tree, referring to Ms. Curry's unruly daughter. That student happened to be Reign Curry—a ball of thunder loaded into a little pistol. If given the task, Reign could run the devil straight out of hell. She had a mouth and temperament that warranted a daily medicinal slap, and she always had to have the last word. But she would never have the last one with Amber, and the day she tried it was the day she went head-to-head with her Latino nemesis.

Amber was feisty at five-three, one hundred fifteen pounds. She was a New York native. Her father had served many years as a correctional officer for Rikers Island Correctional Facility. She was no joke, and she ruled her students and men with an iron fist. So, when Mrs. Curry tried to tell Amber that her daughter was merely "acting out of frustration," Amber saw fit to cuss her out in Spanish and English! She didn't sugarcoat her belief that Reign was a mess because she had been spoiled rotten. She openly faulted Ms. Curry for allowing her daughter to throw tantrums and mouth off to her at home.

Amber bashed Ms. Curry, "Take responsibility for your child's freggin' actions! Stop letting her boss you with that flippant mouth! She's a spoiled smart-ass, and you're afraid to parent her! She's a child, and you should make her act like one!" By the time Amber finished her verbal assault, Ms. Curry and Reign were both crying like newborn babies.

Ms. Curry countered with her speech on how she just wanted to make up for all the things that had gone wrong in Reign's life, mostly as a result of the emotional damage caused by Reign's father neglecting her. She spoke of how she was forced to work day and night just to survive and live a decent middle-class life.

Crying to Amber, she explained, "Yes! Reign has always been the center of my world because of all the times I couldn't be with her. I have always felt like she was yearning for my love or searching for something I didn't give her."

That incident ultimately converted Ms. Curry, Amber, and Reign into one big happy family. Reign began spending two or three nights a week at Amber's place. The two would go shopping, to the movies, roller skating, and do all the fun stuff teens enjoyed. Amber had wrapped Reign in a shroud of love and compassion, refusing to let go.

Amber felt sympathy for Reign because she knew what it was like to be the center of attention but still need more. Amber was able to give Reign that extra something she craved. It softened Reign, and she grew to be like any other teenager. She still had her problem areas. Her mouthiness was a bigger pill to swallow, but that, too, had improved drastically.

Kennedy was still troubled by Lexi's condition and wanted to find a way to help her without sounding like a mother hen.

"Lexi, really, if you're not feeling that great, I can even watch your class myself."

"No, I have a responsibility to my kids. They'll be wondering where I am."

Both Amber and Alexis took great pride in their work and clearly felt a sense of obligation to the kids of Crimson Heights.

Especially Alexis: she was remarkably spiritual, but not so holy that she was of no earthly good. Although she didn't drink, she knew she was guilty of committing other sins, like gossiping and gluttony. It made her human, and she never forced her views on others. But she was quick to quote the Bible, and most would shy away from arguing against what's written in it. At the same time, Alexis knew how to not be judgmental toward her girls, knowing they were still developing spiritually.

Kennedy and Alexis had both grown up in the church and were very staunch in their beliefs, but they struggled to manage different sins. Alexis married at twenty-two and never really dealt with being single and dating. She bypassed the temptation of hitting nightclubs and found contentment at home. Kennedy, in contrast, prowled the clubs looking for men like a cat hunting mice.

Changing the subject and hoping to see that gleam return to Lexi's eyes, Kennedy conveniently whipped out a compliment, "Well, you may not be feeling too hot, but God has blessed you. You look great for a gal who's almost thirty, and I'm sure dancing every day doesn't hurt. Maybe I need to give up the gym and get back to dancing."

"You? Give up the gym? Yeah right, Kennedy."

"Speaking of which, Lexi, I saw this fine man there yesterday."

"Did you get his name?"

"No. You know my rules. No fraternizing at the gym."

"Kennedy, you're going to miss out on something special if you don't condense your encyclopedia of dating rules."

"I don't think it's possible to miss out on what's meant to be. Maybe I'll see him again, but chil', that brutha was so fine! Now, that was one I'll break a rule or two for. By the way, Amber and I are going out Friday, you down?"

"Where you going?"

"Probably to dinner and dancing at our usual, Ruby's."

"Sounds like a plan, but I'll have to get back with you. Is Reagan going?"

"I haven't asked her yet, but I'm sure she will at least meet us for dinner."

"Yep. You know she ain't missing no meals. But I'll let you know if I can make it."

"Okay, do that. And if you don't feel like teaching class later, just give me a shout and I'll take care of it for you."

"Sure, Kennedy. Good looking out."

CHAPTER 3

Two Peas in a Pod

Kayla and Reign were inseparable best friends and both students at Crimson Heights. They had a lot in common but a lot of differences, too. Kayla was always willing to lend a hand when it came to helping with little things around Crimson, but all Reign wanted to do was sing.

Kennedy was surveying the halls looking for Kayla. The kids were being their usual curious and mischievous selves. Word had already spread that Ms. Kennedy was on the hunt for Kayla for something having to do with Ms. Alexis being sick. It was obvious to Reign that Kennedy's mind was elsewhere as she swiftly walked past.

"Hey, Ms. Kennedy."

"Hey, Reign. How's it going?"

"I'm fine, and yourself?"

"Good, thanks." Then, quickly shifting her attention to Kayla, Kennedy said, "Hi, young lady. How's your day going?"

"So far, so good. Just hanging around until Ms. Amber starts class. Ugh!"

"What's the 'ugh' for, Kayla?"

"Ms. Kennedy, you know how Ms. Amber can be."

"How?"

"A little abrasive."

"Well, today is your lucky day. I may need you to cover Ms. Alexis' class if she doesn't get to feeling better. But I'll have to let Ms. Amber know, so you can be excused."

"For real? That sounds good to me! I'll do anything to get extra time in the dance studio."

"Yeah right, Kayla. I think you'll do anything to get out of voice."

"Okay, you got me, Ms. Kennedy. You know I love Ms. Amber, but she can be a little Simon Cowellish when it comes to giving feedback on those missed notes. So, can you please get me excused from her class, pleeeeease?"

"I can't promise anything, Kayla, but I'll check with Ms. Amber to see if she will make an exception for today."

"Thanks, Ms. Kennedy. I'll be waiting!"

"All right, girls, I'll be in my office if anyone needs me. And, Reign, I'll probably need your help with the five-year-olds' song for the recital."

"No problem, Ms. Kennedy. I'm always willing to sing."

"Thanks, Reign. Thanks to you, too, Kayla!" Kennedy shouted over one shoulder as she headed back to her office.

"Hello. Hey, Todd!" Reign said enthusiastically, answering her cell phone on the last ring. "What's up?" Kayla was staring at her like she had three eyes and a horn in the center of her forehead.

"Remember, Reign, what happens in the dark always comes to the light," Kayla whispered.

"What does that mean? And stop looking at me like that, fool. You're creeping me out!" Reign continued her phone conversation as Kayla maintained her menacing gaze. Todd was asking if he could see Reign later.

"I don't know if I can."

"If you can what, Reign?" Kayla asked in protest.

"Kayla! Chill out!"

"You can what?" Kayla pressed.

"Kayla, be quiet! Todd, let me call you back later." Pressing her phone's end button so hard she broke the tip of her nail, Reign shrilled at Kayla, "Why do you insist on asking me questions while I'm on the phone?"

"Apparently, I wanted an answer! Reign, straight up, what's your problem?"

"Who said I had a problem, Kayla?"

"Obviously you do, because I'm sitting right next to you, asking you questions, and you acting like you don't hear me."

"I heard you, but I was on the phone! Don't you know when you're being ignored?"

"Yeah, my point—you were on the phone and now you're off. I want to know, can you what?" Kayla inquired a third time.

"Whatever, Kayla. You'll understand when you get a boyfriend,"

"Oh! So now this Todd boy is your boyfriend?"

"Damn, Skippy! You got a problem with that?" Reign asked as Kayla just stared through her.

"Not at all, Reign." She rolled her eyes and continued, "Do you even know what school that boy goes to?"

"For your information, Todd is a senior at Collaborative."

"Isn't Collaborative for kids who got kicked out of regular public school?"

"Yeah, Kayla. And?"

"I mean, what good is he, if he's at Collaborative?"

"Plenty good."

"How you know, Reign? What does he plan to do after graduation?"

"He doesn't know. He's finding himself and figuring all that stuff out."

"See! That's a big red warning light that you need to leave him alone. Any senior that doesn't know what he wants to do is headed in the direction of becoming a statistic."

"Says who, Kayla?"

"Every scholar out there! Even the Bible says, 'In all things have understanding,' and Todd has none!"

"You really get on my nerves sometimes."

"Watch yourself, Reign. Remember what the serpent told Eve in the garden, 'Just eat the fruit; you shall surely not die.' And look what happened! Todd might be that same serpent Eve ran up on."

"Kayla, you make me want to scream to the top of my voice when you try to tell me what to do. Stop acting like such a know-it-all!" Reign yelled, as she stomped away to Ms. Kennedy's office.

"Hey, Ms. Kennedy. What time is the five-year-old rehearsal?"

"From six 'til seven tomorrow afternoon. Can you help, Reign?" Kennedy asked.

"Uh…uh, I have something to do."

"What do you have to do?"

Reign hesitated. She couldn't tell Ms. Kennedy that she was ditching her to meet Todd. She would be disappointed, and probably tell Ms. Amber. Reign didn't want to face that, especially after all they had done for her. Instead, she made a split decision to cancel with Todd and prayed he would understand.

"You're right, Ms. Kennedy. I don't have anything to do. I'll be there."

"Great. Thank you, Reign. The music sheet for the class is in Ms. Amber's top drawer. The children's parents will be bringing them in for this special rehearsal, and since Ms. Amber has to work with her regularly scheduled class, I'll really need your help. So, please don't let me down."

"I won't. You can count on me, Ms. Kennedy."

Kennedy gave Reign a big hug as she often did with her Crimson kids. It was her own way of letting them know how much she cared.

Reign left Kennedy's office and immediately returned Todd's call. "Hey, Todd."

"What's up, boo?"

"Nothing. I need to reschedule our date for tomorrow. I have to help out at Crimson, so I won't be able to make it."

"Oh, ma, don't worry about it. I can find something else to get into, but I was really looking forward to spending some time with you. You know, just the two of us, hanging out at the mall, holding hands. And maybe if I got lucky, you would let me kiss those sweet, soft lips of yours."

"Really, you were going to take me to the mall?"

"Yeah, baby. Anything for you, Reign."

"Maybe we can go another day."

"Fa sho. Like I said, baby, it's cool. Don't sweat it. I'll wait on you, but just know I'll be thinking about you. Make sure you're thinking about me, too."

"I will, Todd," Reign whispered girlishly. "Bye."

"Bye, little mama."

CHAPTER 4

Girls' Night Out

It was six o'clock, and Reagan would be arriving at Kennedy's house in less than an hour. Late was not a part of her vernacular. She was always on time, and if she said she would be somewhere at a certain hour, you could put your money on it.

She and Kennedy had planned to meet Amber and Alexis at seven thirty. It was Friday night, which meant dinner and dancing at Ruby's and Pearl's. It wasn't a typical restaurant, more of a jazz meets hip-hop meets blues kind of setup, and every Friday night was open mic. After a few glasses of wine, the girls would be ready to show out. Like most artists, being creative and performing came naturally to them. It was not uncommon for them to get so hyped on a Friday night that they would start to resemble the characters from an episode of *Fame*. Reagan was always Debbie Allen because she thought she was the boss. Kennedy was Coco, ready to show the world what she was made of. Amber and Lexi were just extras, but sometimes, Amber would take her role of an extra a little too seriously and try to upstage a main cast member. It was all in good fun.

Ruby's was a bit disappointing in the available bachelor department, but so was most of Cleveland, for that matter. The same people traveled in the same small circles. The only redeeming thing about Ruby's was that the men were always well dressed: businessmen wearing either a suit or a nice pair of slacks with a shirt and tie—always complemented by a fresh pair of Kenneth Cole footgear. On occasion, there were those who topped off their apparel with a dapper pair of Gucci loafers, but that was seldom.

On any given night, you could find professional athletes from the Cavs, Indians, and Browns perched in the VIP section. It was where Kennedy had met her last wannabe playa, Mack Daddy. He played for the Cavs and thought he was the bee's knees. Needless to say, he had more problems going on with him than a 1985 recalled Yugo. After their breakup (as with all of her exes), they had later managed to become friends. It was pretty much the cycle of Kennedy's dating life—first lovers, then friends, instead of the preferred reverse order.

Kennedy still needed to shower and go through her ritualistic debate of what she would wear. Would it be dress to impress or a more chilled vibe? She decided on a look that fell between the two in case she stumbled across her Mr. Right. The older she got, the more the club scene had become a place for relaxing and hanging out with her girls. The meeting-single-eligible-men hype was overrated. In fact, finding a man in a club was the worst of possibilities, seeing that none had ever turned out quite right for her.

Kennedy opted for her Apple Bottom jeans that perfectly accentuated the curve of her round butt. Thank God for Nelly! He seemed to be the first designer to create a pair of jeans that fit a black woman's waist, hips, and voluptuous rear end. Kennedy loved Nelly and his jeans, but he was just a tad too short for her taste in men. Nothing like a tall man to accessorize a sexy pair of stilettos.

Kennedy pumped up the volume on her iPod as she started to get in the mood to get her TGIF on. She liked getting dressed to music and setting the mood for an evening out. A little Destiny's Child was always the right antidote. She was listening to "Soldier," secretly believing she would find one that night.

She turned up her favorite part (even louder) and sang along with Michelle, "I like them boys over there; they looking strong tonight…Just might give one the phone tonight…Homie in the Dickies in my zone tonight…He don't know it might be on tonight…Oh, he looking good and he talking right…He the type that might change my life . . ."

Nothing like a man who was a true soldier—an articulate man with real game. The kind of man who could change a woman's life. Unfortunately, it wasn't always a favorable change. A smooth-talking brother had the power to melt Kennedy like butter. For her, game was an important quality in a man, but she kept running across so many who lacked it. No woman wanted a weak brother who didn't have charisma or the goods to woo her.

"Who is it?" Kennedy yelled out to a ringing doorbell.

"Reagan! Who the hell else are you expecting?"

"Come in. The door is unlocked."

"I don't know why I even rang the bell. Everyone knows you leave your door unlocked. Not a good thing to have known as common knowledge, Kennedy."

"Yeah, I know it's a habit I need to break. But, there's twenty-four-hour security patrol throughout the subdivision."

Reagan and Kennedy lived in similar developments about twenty-five minutes from downtown Cleveland. Reagan had discovered The Litmus Development Group and turned Kennedy on to them. They were black-owned and operated. As an African-American, Kennedy went out of her way to support black businesses. And Litmus built beautiful, well-crafted homes. It was a win-win in her eyes.

"Reagan, would you like a glass of Riesling while I finish getting dressed?"

"Would I? Yes, girl!"

"There's some chilling on ice in the kitchen."

"Girl, look how much work you've done to this place!"

"It's hard coming up with ideas, though, when you want every room to look different."

"Seems like you're doing all right. The whole place looks awesome."

"Reagan, are you walking around my house?"

"Kennedy, you know I'm as nosy as Colombo."

"Go ahead, girl, and check out the place. Look at the elephant on the floor in my office. I bought it at our sorority convention last July."

"Girl, this elephant is the bomb. I forgot you went to the convention without me last year!"

"You're the one who had 'previous commitments' with your husband."

"Kennedy, look at this wallpaper! Wow, it's gorgeous."

"Thanks, Reagan!" Kennedy yelled from the bathroom.

"What are you going to do with all this stuff when you find a husband?"

"Hopefully, he'll appreciate my taste in interior design."

There was no way in hell Kennedy was waiting for a husband to get the things she desired in life. House. Car. Expensive décor. Whatever she wanted and had the money to buy—she bought it. Not to be confused with her not wanting a husband, because she had always dreamed of when that day would come. She just didn't need a man to take care of her. Years earlier, she would constantly ponder whether she should wait to make big purchases until marriage, but she reconciled knowing she worked hard and deserved the things she wanted. She felt like waiting to live out any dream was unhealthy.

"It's cool that you and Ryan were able to make those big decisions and purchases together, but my life hasn't worked out that way. I'll be damned if I'll sit and wait on a man. Anyway, who do I always tell you is my role model—and half of America's, for that matter?"

"Jesus Christ?"

"I didn't ask who is my Savior. I asked who is my role model."

"Oooh! Duh, Oprah!"

"Thank you! Has she ever given the impression that she was sitting around, twiddling her thumbs, waiting on a man? I don't think so! Gotta love that woman."

"I know one thing, Ms. Oprah Jr., if you don't hurry up, I'm leaving you and you'll have the whole night to catch up on old Oprah episodes."

"I'm ready," Kennedy exclaimed, sashaying into the kitchen. She had already had a couple glasses of wine, so she was feeling pretty relaxed and set for the night.

"If every man I ever dated could see me now."

"What?" asked Reagan.

"Each would say, 'Kennedy. Darling Kennedy. I should never have let you go.' And I would say, you're so right, but it's too late. I've moved on, so you can just feast your eyes on all this that you're missing. Bam!"

"Girl, only you!" Reagan said with a smile plastered on her face.

"That's what makes me a superstar, Reagan."

"Okay, superstar. Did you do something different with your makeup or hair?"

"It's all in the hair, Reagan. Just a few extra pieces. Nothing like a little horsetail enhancement to set off the look."

Kennedy had shoulder-length hair, and adding a little length and fullness gave her a striking resemblance to Beyoncé. She was bootylicious and all.

"And look at you, Ms. Class Act. I should've known you would have on something black, Reagan."

For the last few years, since her weight gain, Reagan always wore black on girls' night out. The color perfectly camouflaged all her bumps and rolls. She had a very cultivated style and looked great in whatever she wore.

Kennedy's wardrobe and color selections changed according to the kind of hair day she was having. She and Amber also favored clothing that fit their bodies and showed off their curves, while Reagan and Lexi were considerably conservative.

"Oh Lord, Reagan, I thought you were ready to go?"

"I am. Just let me take this last sip. No need to waste a perfectly good gulp of Riesling."

Finally, dressed and out of the house, Reagan and Kennedy headed off to meet Amber and Alexis at Ruby's. Just as they pulled in, they were greeted by Johnny.

"Hey, Johnny. You take good care of my car now. Okay?"

"You know I gotcha, Reagan." Johnny was the valet guy at Ruby's, and he had the cutest southern drawl.

"Ms. Kennedy. Excuse my frankness, but gurl, you looking aight tonight!" Since the ladies were frequent customers, Johnny knew all of them on a first-name basis.

"Thanks, Johnny," Kennedy said, pausing just long enough to look back and wink.

"Amber and Alexis are already inside. Enjoy yourselves, ladies."

The atmosphere at Ruby's was always the same, warm and friendly, like the bar in *Cheers*, and everybody knew your name.

"Hey, Anthony." He was the owner of Ruby's and Pearl's, and had named the restaurant to commemorate his late grandmothers. Kennedy found the idea sweet and thoughtful. She believed men who were close to their mothers and grandmothers were more likely to be emotionally available husbands. Too bad Anthony was already taken, and his wife was always propped in a corner at the bar. Kennedy didn't blame her, because if her husband owned a club she would be there every night on surveillance, too. Waiting tables. Making drinks. It didn't matter; she would've done whatever was necessary to make her presence felt. Not out of a lack of trust for him, but other women. She knew there was a grade of women who didn't give a damn. A man could have a wife, mistress, girlfriend, and a fiancée—and she would still be trying to get a place on the team.

"Ladies. Y'all killing 'em tonight!"

"Thanks, Anthony," Kennedy beamed, accepting the compliment for the group.

"Kennedy, there's Lexi and Amber over there," Reagan pointed.

"Is Lexi eating again, Reagan?"

"Looks like it. That girl has been eating a whole lot lately. Heeeeey, Lexi. Hey, Amber," Reagan greeted the girls, quickly changing the topic from Lexi's eating.

"Hey, Kennedy. What's up, Reagan?" Lexi mumbled through a mouth full of fried chicken.

"Lexi, you've been eating a lot recently," Kennedy said, stealing one of her fries.

"I've just been really hungry," Lexi said, stuffing several fries down her throat.

"OMG! Kennedy, isn't that James?" Amber pointed with the couth of a 5-year-old.

"Oh, hell naw. It sure is. Did he see me?"

"I guess so. He's headed this way," Amber teased, with her chin tucked into her chest.

"Hi, James."

"Hi, Kennedy. You look ravishing."

"Thanks, I work hard at it."

James was a guy Kennedy had met almost five years before. They dated, it went nowhere fast, and she eventually was repulsed by him. Once a man hit that threshold with Kennedy, it was over. The umbilical cord was cut. No more small talk. Lights out. Nothing. She usually managed to be civil with most guys she dated, but not James. And he was clueless. Seeing him that night was a guarantee that he would be blowing up her phone the next day.

"Do you think I could take you out sometime?"

Forget tomorrow, this fool is asking the same night, Kennedy thought to herself. "I don't think so, James. I'm just not interested anymore."

"Why? I just don't get it. I'm still the same person you met five years ago. I haven't changed."

"Bingo! And that's exactly the problem," Kennedy said, looking away.

"Can I just call you then and keep in touch?" he asked, like a man who had lost his best friend.

"Bye, James. Enjoy the rest of your life," Kennedy emphasized as he walked away.

"Awwww, Kennedy, looks like you had a spark in your eyes while you were talking to James," Amber teased.

"Your momma! I should kick your ass. You probably told him I was coming tonight."

"Girl, sit down and shut up. You know I don't play like that," Amber asserted.

"Hey, sexy. How you feeling tonight?" Reagan asked Lexi, shifting the energy at the table.

"Much better than the other day. I'm thinking it was something I ate."

"Well, you must be making up for lost time, 'cause you eating your ass off."

"What about you, Amber? What's going on with you?" Reagan asked.

"Girl, I'm ready to get my groove on. Tonight may be the night that he looking good and talking right. Shoot, that brother just might change my life!" Amber replied, stealing the words from Kennedy's anthem song.

"Okay, so Amber's joining Kennedy's hunting games for a soldier," Reagan joked.

"Kennedy, where he at? Where he at?" Amber sang, snapping her fingers. "I don't know what it is about them bruthas who have a pinch of hood in them—but it turns me on," Amber confessed.

"Anything turns you on, Amber: hood bruthas, ugly bruthas, corny bruthas, and dumb bruthas—as long as they got money they eligible for your draft," Kennedy poked.

"You damn right. A brother gotta be balling if he wanna ride in this Benz," Amber referred to herself.

"So now you a car?" Kennedy asked mockingly.

"Yep, a damn good one, too. Don't hate cause you an Odyssey minivan.

"That's a compliment. At least I'm dependable through any kind of weather. If a guy is rich, middle class, fine, or mediocre—I'm the girl that will brave the storm with him."

"You forgot to include *broke* in your list of adjectives, Kennedy, and I think we both know that wasn't a mistake. Even minivans can't run on fumes. Don't they take premium octane?" Amber continued, "Kennedy, have you ever thought that maybe it's the thrill of the challenge for me?"

"What challenge?" Kennedy asked, confused.

"The challenge of narrowly dating men with money. Do you know how hard it is to get a brother to spend his money on you? It's half the battle!"

"Amber, I know that, but being a strong woman means you need a strong man who won't let you steamroll him or dictate how he spends his money. It's okay if he's flexible and lets you have your way in those moments when you're craving the need to be spoiled."

"Say that, girl!" Reagan blurted. "There's nothing like a strong man who knows how to give on the little things and pamper a woman.

"Like Ryan?" Lexi asked.

"Damn right. My husband is definitely filed under that category! Who wants a man who does everything you demand? A man needs to be a man, but he also needs to feel like his woman supports him in taking charge. Even if he wants to pick her ass up, swing her over his shoulders, and werk!"

"Ewwww, Reagan, I didn't know you had freak tendencies."

"I do, and proud of it, honey. Every woman has a little freak in her, even if it's just with her husband. Can I get an amen, Lexi?"

"I will definitely give you an amen on that one, sista," Amber said, high fiving Reagan.

"Real woman talk though, Amber, getting freaky with your husband is fair game, but not every Tom, Dick, and Harry."

"I don't get busy with every Tom, Dick, and Harry—just every Antwan, Dejuan, and Lamario. And ain't nothing wrong with being freaky and knowing what you want. Ladies, that's the problem. Most women don't know what they want. When a man says he doesn't want a relationship, we pretend like it's cool, even though we know good and damn well we're looking to lock a husband down. Don't get me wrong, not all women are that way, but I see a lot who are, myself included. Lying, tell guys, 'No, huntey, I'm cool with no commitment. I'm not looking for a relationship either.' Two weeks in, I be all up in my feelings, wanting him all to myself. Nowadays, I just put it out there from go, 'Hell yeah, I'm looking for a commitment, but that doesn't mean I'm looking for one with you' is what I tell 'em."

"Amber, girl ..." Kennedy laughed.

"Kennedy, I'm for real. Try it sometime."

"You ladies need anything else?" their waitress asked, aborting the conversation.

"Yes, can I get some peach cobbler?" Lexi asked sheepishly under her breath.

"Damn, Lexi."

"What, Reagan? I'm hungry."

"Whatever, Lexi. On another topic, have you decided where you want to have your birthday party?"

"I was thinking if we had something in Crimson's ballroom we could celebrate with the kids during the day and have the adult party that night," Lexi said.

"Sounds good to me. Amber and Kennedy, what do you think?" Reagan asked.

"That's cool with me," Kennedy said. "But who's going to pay the gas and light bill? It costs to operate Crimson."

"Kennedy, shut up!" Reagan screeched.

"No, for real, we can use Crimson. Y'all know I'm down with it."

"My, my, my—Kennedy Johnson. Look at you," a man gushed, demurely approaching their table.

"Rick? You just keep getting finer," Kennedy beamed.

"And so do you, lady. Come on, Kennedy, let's dance."

Breathe, she told herself. Rick had one of those deep, Barry White voices, and his body was like Arnold Schwarzenegger in his heyday. He personified fine. Rick was a true "soldier." He had gold trim around his left fang, drove a Cadillac Escalade, and could talk the panties off a department store mannequin. His fine, no-good behind was the reason Kennedy had taken a celibacy sabbatical. He grabbed Kennedy's hand, led her to the dance floor, wrapped his arms around her tiny waist, and swung her from side to side.

"So how's the season going?" Kennedy asked. "It's been a busy time for me, and I haven't been following the Cavs much this year."

"Everything is cool. We're winning as usual, with Lebron, Jeff, and the new trade I've known since college."

"That's nice. At least you have a real friend from back in the day to kick it with."

"Yeah, it makes working together a lot easier. I know his game and he knows mine."

"Speaking of game, how's your personal one?"

"Which game, Kennedy, on or off the court?"

"On the court!"

"I'm having a good season on the court, but off the court I'm still looking for Mrs. Claus to help make the rest of the season happy and bright."

"Rick, I see you haven't changed an ounce."

"So talk to me, Kennedy. Where's your man?"

"I don't have one. I tell you that every time I see you. You are the reason I put relationships and sex on ice. After dating you, experiencing all the trust issues, and always dealing with some woman in your face—I needed a mental break. Men like you affect a woman's ability to trust. Don't get me wrong, it was great being at the games as your showpiece, attending all the fancy parties, and seeing people react to you just walking into a room. 'Hey, that's Rick from the Cavs.' But I cared more about fidelity and commitment when all you seemed to care about was managing a roster of side chicks. Honestly, I don't think you will ever settle down."

"By the looks of it, neither will you, Kennedy. Ms. Independent. I can do it all by myself," Rick teased.

"That's not my outlook, Rick. I do want a man, but he has to be interested in monogamy and only wants to be with me. I'm not looking for a man who wants me as the entrée but needs five or six side dishes. I am independent, and I can do it on my own if that's how it has to be. But God only knows how much I want to do it with someone I love and care about."

"You think you know me, don't you, Kennedy?"

"Most definitely. That's why we are grown enough to have this conversation. You know I finally peeped your game, and I wasn't having it."

"So you got my technique down?"

"Not all of it, but the main pieces. Speaking of game, Rick, can I get tickets to next week's game so I can peep you courtside?"

"I'll trade you courtside for bedside tickets," Rick negotiated.

"Yeah, right! You wouldn't sleep with me if I threw that thang in your face."

"You're right about that. At this point, I'm afraid to do anything that might jeopardize our friendship. Kennedy, can I be honest with you for a change?"

"You, honest? Right!"

"Seriously, I did find something different in you, but I didn't know how to be faithful. I know that's an immature, irresponsible excuse. But it's the God's honest truth, and I just want you to know that you'll always be special to me."

"I know. Thank for saying it though. Well, my food looks like it's ready. So, let's just pause here and pick up later. Don't forget to leave the tickets at Will Call."

As Kennedy walked back to her table from the dance floor, she reminisced about all the memories with Rick. Since their breakup, they had become civil, even confidants. She could seek his advice on any matter, dating included. Rick was quick to tell her if he thought a brother was up to something, and he never spared her feelings. She knew she could depend on him for anything, but her heart always told her they just weren't meant to be more.

Rick, Rick, Rick, his name played over and over in her head as she sat down in front of her plate of delectable food.

"Girl, that man is fine. I don't know how you're able to resist him," Amber prodded.

"It used to be a struggle, but he's not tempting anymore. I know Rick, and he just isn't boyfriend material. One thing is for sure, though, we'll always be friends."

"Hey, Amber. Wanna dance?" a guy standing in the distance asked impatiently.

"Let me eat first, Paul. Then, I'll come get you."

Amber and Kennedy had both gone through their fair share of men, but without contest, Amber was the heavyweight champion of failed relationships. Kennedy dated quite a bit, but didn't sleep with every man who bought her a large popcorn and 32-ounce Cherry Coke. In contrast, Amber loved sex. It was an outlet for her. She could sleep with a man on Tuesday night, and had forgotten his name by Wednesday morning. As long as he kept the lights on or the water running—he was an eligible contender. All Amber cared about was a man paying her bills.

Neither Amber nor Kennedy were honest enough to admit how grueling and depressing their random dating cycles had become. All the alcohol, lunch, and dinner dates were bad for their waistlines. And the battery of ice-breaker conversations never ceased being awkward. "What's your zodiac sign? What do you like to do? Where are you from? Any kids?" It all felt like a never-ending, stupid game of Jeopardy.

"Oh snap, that's my song!" Reagan squealed, throwing her hands in the air and singing along with her eyes squeezed tightly.

Once Reagan got going, it was on. She would grab the man closest to her and drag him to the dance floor, whether he wanted to be there or not. For the most part, men were happy to be seen on the floor with her. She was thick and irresistible.

The rest of the gang followed suit and strutted to the dance floor. Kennedy grabbed Rick again. Amber snatched up an eagerly awaiting Paul, and Lexi danced like a manic *Soul Train* dancer who had misplaced her partner. She twisted and twirled as men watched in amazement. Lexi was an extraordinary dancer, which made most men petrified to step on the floor with her. Some would take on the challenge, but none could keep up. Most found it safer and more provocative to just sit back and watch.

"Ladies and gentlemen, here tonight in our midst, are the ladies of Crimson Heights," the deejay announced.

Most people knew of Crimson, and with the exception of Reagan (the resident legal guru), most also knew the ladies were natural performers with diverse backgrounds in the arts. Their attendance at a club always came with a free show.

"Hit it, deejay!" Amber roared, singing along to Michael Jackson's "When I Needed You." The other girls joined in and the show began as they danced and sang until Ruby's dance floor was packed.

After what felt like hours of dancing, Lexi bellowed, "I can't believe it's 2:00 a.m.! I'm taking my behind home." Her voice was hoarse from hours of trying to sing above the music. "Amber, you ready, or you catching a ride with Reagan and Kennedy?"

"Nope. I'm ready. Chil', I have ate, drank, sang, and danced enough. I'm sleepy."

"Especially the eating part. Lexi, you ate enough tonight for all of us to be satisfied," Kennedy teased.

"Whatever, Kennedy!" Lexi jokingly snapped.

"We're getting out of here too, girl," said Kennedy. "Reagan, let me make a quick trip to the ladies' restroom and we can go."

"All right, Kennedy. Hurry up."

As Kennedy dragged her aching feet into the bathroom, she heard a voice close in behind her. "Excuse me, ma'am."

She turned around to see who was beckoning for her attention and found herself facing Mr. Universe, the guy from her gym. She managed to spit out a single word, "Hi."

"I don't know if you remember me, but we met the other day at the gym," he said gingerly.

"I remember. You were waiting on my treadmill. Well, not my treadmill, but the treadmill I was using." Kennedy would often get technical and awkward around men she found attractive. It was a natural mechanism that kicked in to conceal her nervousness. "How are you doing?" she asked.

"I'm well. Just wanted to say a quick hello. It's nice seeing you again. Maybe we can get together for lunch or something," he suggested.

"That sounds good, but can I ask you a question?" Kennedy dug.

"Sure."

"What is your name?"

"Oh!" Opening his mouth with a wide smile that was like an oyster revealing an interior of beautiful white pearls he said, "It's Orray. Orray Philips."

"Okay. Did you say Orr-ray or Or-rie?"

"It's Orr-ray. Like Ray Charles."

"Orr-ray Philips. Okay. Hi, I'm Kennedy. Kennedy Johnson."

CHAPTER 5

Where There's Smoke, There's Fire

*K*ayla and Reign were sitting at the front desk when a delivery man approached.

"Hi, may I help you?" Kayla asked.

"I have a delivery."

"It's probably the shipment Ms. Kennedy has been waiting for."

"Nope, it's a floral arrangement," he replied.

"Wow, flowers! Who are they for?" Kayla grilled.

"These are for a … Kennedy Johnson. Can you make sure she gets them?"

"Sure, I'll take them right to her office," Kayla assured, racing Reign to Kennedy's office.

"Ms. Kennedy, gueeeeeess what? We have a delivery for you." Kayla entered her office smiling like a Cheshire cat.

"If it's a supply shipment, just put it in the storage closet," Kennedy instructed without looking up.

"I don't think this delivery will do too well in a closet, Ms. Kennedy," Kayla said, setting a spectacular assortment of colored roses on Kennedy's desk.

Finally looking up, Kennedy discovered three dozen red, pink, white, and yellow roses illuminating her desk. She smiled. "Wow! I wonder who these are from. I haven't met anyone lately or been on any dates. I hope he's cute."

"Somebody must think you're the bomb! Who are they from? Open the card, Ms. Kennedy!" Kayla shrilled hastily.

"Kayla, you're worse than the old woman sitting on the front porch, checking for who's going in and out of her neighbor's house."

Kennedy obliged her curiosity by reading the attached card aloud, "It was a pleasure running into you, Kennedy. Kennedy Johnson. Looking forward to our lunch date, Orray."

"Orray? Who's that, Ms. Kennedy?"

"Kayla, don't you have some work to do?"

"No."

"Isn't it time for class?"

"No, ma'am."

"Well, I think I hear Ms. Amber calling you... and Reign."

"Ms. Kennedy! No you don't!"

"Kayla!"

"Okay, okay, I know. Stay outta grown folks' business."

"Come on, Kayla. Let's give Ms. Kennedy some space," Reign said respectfully, shoving Kayla toward the door.

"Un uh. I'm staying. I wanna know who Orray is."

"Bye, Kayla. Bye, Reign," Kennedy sweetly asserted.

Kayla and Reign slowly returned to the front desk while looking over their shoulders at Kennedy pining over her delivery.

"I can't believe Ms. Kennedy got all those roses. And who is this guy, Orray? I ain't never heard or seen her with no Orray," Reign said.

"You act like you know everybody's business. Ms. Kennedy don't tell you everything, girl."

Kayla and Reign attended Crimson together, went to the same church, and high school. They also shared a love for music—both singing in the church and school gospel choir. Kayla regularly competed in dance competitions, and took pride in serving on the Praise Dance Ministry. She was more into dance than Reign, which explained why Amber's classes gave her the heebie-jeebies. She was either in school, working at Crimson, or dancing. It was all a part of Kennedy's mission for students, and modeled her mother's philosophy of: Keep 'em involved in everything, and they won't have time for ill things. Kennedy's mom always believed that kids who stayed occupied in positive activities were less tempted to get involved in sex, drugs, and alcohol.

"How's the dance piece coming along for your recital?" Reign asked Kayla.

"I'm having a hard time putting together combinations. Maybe you can help me out next week."

"Sure, if I don't have plans with Todd," Kayla mumbled under her breath.

"Todd? You still messing with him?"

"Yep. He actually came over last night."

"How did that happen?"

"My mother had to work late. When he called, I invited him over."

"I can't believe you had that boy in your house, alone."

"Kayla, I'm sixteen. That's old enough to have company. You act so old sometimes."

"Okay, Reign. Just keep it up. You know being alone with a boy usually leads to... you know."

"Sex, and true that! I was tempted last night, and anyway, he's not a boy!"

"Tempted how, Reign?"

"Todd and I have been talking on the phone past midnight a lot lately."

"Your momma let you talk on the phone late like that?"

"She's usually so tired from working that she passes out as soon as she hits the door. She doesn't know I'm on the phone."

Reign's mother gave birth to her when she was barely fifteen, and had always struggled to nurture and provide for Reign. But as a single parent of an only child, she spent a lot of time away from home, often leaving Reign unsupervised.

"What do you and Todd talk about all that time on the phone?" Kayla asked.

"We usually start with highlights from our favorite television shows, but the conversation always leads to sex. When we start talking about sex, I get this tingling sensation between my legs and my nipples get hard. I can feel my inner thighs throbbing, too. Then, I start imagining him on top of me, and wondering what it would feel like."

"That's nothing but lust, Reign."

"What do you know about lust, Kayla?"

"Enough to know that tingling between the legs leads to sex!"

"Can you just be quiet and let me finish my story, Kayla?"

"Go right ahead."

"A few days ago, he asked me if I was a virgin. I told him I was. Then, I asked him the same question, and he said he was, too."

"Let me guess what happened next. The virgin asked if the two of you could lose your virginity together."

"Yes."

"Oh my God! You really believe Todd is an eighteen-year-old virgin? Reign, please."

"Yes, I believe him! Why wouldn't I?"

"Get real, Reign! That boy ain't no virgin! He lied 'cause he trying to get some."

"Anyway, last night when he came over, we sat and watched TV for a minute, ate a pizza, and then things got a little frisky. He was kissing on my neck, ears, and shoulders. After a while, he was rubbing between my legs, and eventually unbuttoned my jeans. But I stopped, and told him I wasn't ready."

"Y'all didn't do nothing?"

"Nothing, but I'm getting hot right now thinking about it."

"Reign, you're playing with fire. You're gonna have sex with Todd if you keep putting yourself in that situation. Just watch."

"I know. But I really like him."

"Then find things to do outside of the house."

"Like what?"

"Go to the movies. Take a walk in the park."

"We could still do the nasty in the movies or at the park."

"I can't believe you would do something like that in public."

"I know plenty of girls who have, Kayla."

"Kayla!" Kennedy yelled from her office, bringing their heated conversation to a halt.

"Yes, Ms. Kennedy."

"Have you seen Ms. Alexis or Ms. Amber today?"

"No, they haven't gotten in yet."

"As soon as they get here, tell them I need to see them."

"Okay. Oh, I see Ms. Amber pulling up now, Ms. Kennedy."

"Reign, you better be careful," Kayla warned, trying to pick up where they'd left off.

"I'm good, Kayla."

Amber strutted inside from the parking lot dressed to the nines. "Hey, ladies. Give me my hug. What's up, Reign? I thought you were going to come by last night so I could help you with your math."

"I was, but I got tied up."

"You're only sixteen; what could have tied you up?"

"More like bound up," muttered Kayla.

"What'd you say, Kayla?" Amber asked.

"Nothin', Ms. Amber. I was just tryin' to tell you that Ms. Kennedy needs to see you in her office."

"Thanks, Kayla. Reign, will I see you later tonight?"

"Yes, Ms. Amber."

CHAPTER 6

Special Delivery

*K*ennedy looked up to find Amber standing in her office doorway. "Come in. I've been waiting for you to get here."

"What's up?"

"Do you remember Orray, the hot guy I met at the gym who showed up at Ruby's last weekend?

"Yeah."

"Girl, he sent me three dozen roses today!"

"Kennedy done whipped up some voodoo on the man," said Amber.

"I don't even know how he knows where I work. I gave him my cell phone number, but I didn't tell him anything about what I do for a living."

"He could have looked you up."

"First of all, there are too many Kennedy Johnsons listed in the directory. It would be almost impossible to find me. Not to mention, the directory assistance doesn't share where a person works."

"Maybe he knows someone who works for the police station."

"That would make him a lightweight stalker," said Kennedy.

"Well, if he's a stalker, at least he's one with good taste in roses. And just think how pretty the ones will be at your burial."

"That's not funny at all, Amber."

Kennedy had been stalked before, and had to get a restraining order on a crazy ex-boyfriend. Stalking was a topic that lacked humor, in her opinion.

"Kennedy, you wanted to see me?" Lexi asked, appearing in her doorway out of nowhere, her eyes gazing at the arrangement on Kennedy's desk. "Whoa! Who sent you those?"

"That guy I met at the gym. We're wondering how he figured out where I work."

"Kennedy, it's not like he couldn't have asked someone at Ruby's."

"I guess you have a point, Lexi. Didn't think about that."

"Have you told Reagan about the roses?" Lexi asked.

"Of course! I called her, and she was all crazy, talking about how romantic it was for him to send flowers after only our second encounter. She was like, 'That man's got game.' I guess it's kind of sweet, but what man actually still sends flowers? He even addressed me in the card the same way I introduced myself to him. At least I know his memory works, so I don't have to worry about him forgetting anniversaries, birthdays, and special dates."

"Roses are so romantic; they are a sure way to open a woman's heart."

"Alexis, you're getting as bad as Reagan. Roses are nothing more than a strategic move in a man's playbook. They know how much women like surprises. That's why they always give roses for apologies—it's game, ladies. Chapter one, page one of the game handbook."

"You just can't appreciate chivalry from a man, Kennedy."

"That's not true, Lexi. I very much appreciate the roses, but I've been single a lot longer than you, and I'm very familiar with the heartless tactics men use to sweep a woman off her feet and get into her panties. But these panties are closed for business. If Orray knew my panties were on lockdown, these roses would still probably be on a vine."

"Girl, he wouldn't have sent a half-dozen carnations," Amber laughed.

"Ain't that the truth? Hell, I probably wouldn't have even gotten a darned dandelion."

"You need to get past all your unproven theories, Kennedy. Give the man a chance. His sending roses could actually be a sincere gesture," Alexis interjected.

"I'll let you and Reagan keep living in your fantasy world, believing that other sincere men exist, besides Ray and Ryan."

"Whatever. When is your lunch date, anyway?" Alexis inquired.

"Who knows? I haven't talked to my alleged stalker yet."

Kennedy's speaker phone buzzed. "Ms. Kennedy, you have a call holding on that blinking line," said Kayla.

Picking up the call, Kennedy answered, "This is Ms. Johnson. How may I help you?"

"Ms. Johnson?" an amazingly sensual baritone voice uttered from the other end.

"Yes."

"Well, it would have been really helpful had I been able to see the smile on your face when you got my roses."

"Who said I smiled?" Kennedy asked, playing coy.

"Well, did you?"

"Your flowers were lovely. But don't flowers usually come *after* the first date?"

"See, that's what makes me different. I'm not good at following rules."

Okay, maybe he does have game, Kennedy thought. "Really, Orray, I can't express how much I appreciate the flowers. Thank you so much."

"No problem. If you like what I have to offer, there'll be plenty to follow."

Damn, damn, damn. Roses and skillful game had a way of breaking Kennedy down. "Can you excuse me for a moment, girls?" she asked, covering the mouthpiece of her phone. Not budging from their positions, Lexi and Amber were standing close enough to hear every word Orray spoke. Realizing they were intent on hearing the rest of her conversation, Kennedy insisted they leave. "Hey, Frick and Frack! Get out of here. I'll fill you in later."

Returning to her call she said, "Thanks for waiting, Orray. I'd like to ask you a question."

"Go for it."

"How'd you know where I work?"

"A friend of mine who was also at Ruby's the night we crossed paths. I asked him if he knew you, and he told me you were Crimson Heights' executive director. Come on now. You know a man knows how to get the 4-1-1 on a woman he wants to holler at. I had to check you out."

"What else did you find out?"

"No much more, but I know there has to be a crazy side to you, like most light-skinned women."

"What? I think that's called stereotyping. Besides, I wouldn't say crazy; maybe a little off, but certainly not crazy." Kennedy laughed flirtatiously.

"You know, Ms. Johnson, I love your sense of humor. When can I get my lunch date with you?"

"How about Wednesday?"

"Can we make it Thursday? I have an engagement out of town this Wednesday, and I won't get in until late Wednesday night."

"Thursday is fine."

"Where would you like to go?"

"How about Rosario's Café, uptown? Do you know where that is?"

"I haven't been there before, but I'm sure I can find it."

"Okay. How's one o'clock, Mr. Phillips?"

"One o'clock it is. Well, until then you stay sweet, and enjoy the rest of your week, Ms. Johnson."

"Bye-bye, Orray."

"Bye."

Kennedy buzzed Kayla at the front desk as soon as she disconnected her call. "Kayla, ask Ms. Amber and Ms. Alexis to come back to my office, please."

"Actually, they're standing right outside of your door, Ms. Kennedy."

"Come on in, Nosey Nellies!" Kennedy yelled into the hallway.

"Okay, what's the low down?" Amber prodded in her New York accent.

"Yeah, when is lunch?" Lexi added.

"Lunch is Thursday at one o'clock. Rosarios."

"Oh, that's cool. Very sexy. No one will bother you there," said Amber.

"You think he'll like Rosario's? It's kinda bougie," Lexi second guessed.

"Orray seems really confident. I think he'll be fine," Kennedy replied.

"Kennedy, did you find out what he does? What he drives? Does he have kids? If yes, does he want more? Is he looking for a roll in the sack? Does he want to get married?"

"Amber, are you on crack? It was our first official conversation! You know I didn't give that man the third degree like that."

"The only thing you need to find out is about his Salvation, and if he has a church home." Lexi assured.

"Okay, Mary, mother of Jesus!" Amber taunted, rolling her eyes at Lexi.

"I'm serious, Amber. The only way for a couple to make it is to be spiritually grounded. The last thing any woman needs is a man who is not walking on her same path. The Bible refers to it as being unequally yoked."

"Okay, Mother Theresa and Jezebel," Kennedy said. "Let me go to lunch with him first, and see if I'm even feeling him. I am curious about what he does. Please, God, don't let it be anything illegal."

"Well, maybe you should've just asked, Kennedy. He could sell drugs."

"Alexis is right, Kennedy. He could be a drug lord or part of the mob."

"He did say he had an out-of-town engagement," Kennedy reflected.

"See, Kennedy, that's why you should've asked. No telling what that man does!"

"Lexi, as long as he's got a job, I'm down to see what the brutha is about."

"Yeah, but his job could be illegal, Kennedy."

"I just like to get the question out of the way off the bat. It helps me figure out if a dude is working with dollars or working with cents," said Amber.

"Amber, I've got standards, and I've got rules, but there are just certain questions I won't ask on the first encounter. I've lived long enough to know the truth has a way of telling itself. So just chill, ladies; all things in due time."

CHAPTER 7

Cherry Pop

"Thanks for inviting me over," Todd said.

"I didn't invite you over."

"Yes, you did, Reign."

"No, I didn't."

"Oh, so when you said your mother would be working late, that wasn't an invitation?"

"No."

"It sounded like one to me."

"Well, it wasn't."

"Invitation. Get it, Reign?"

"No. Conversation, get it, Todd?"

"Yeah, I got it! Why you so uptight, boo?"

"No big deal; you're already here."

"That's what I'm talkin' 'bout. Let's make the best of it. What time your peeps coming home?"

"My momma's working late, so sometime between midnight and one."

"What does she do?"

"She's a pediatric nurse."

"What's that?" Todd asked, knitting his eyebrows in confusion.

"A nurse that takes care of children." *Is this boy an idiot?* she wondered. At eighteen, who doesn't know the definition of a pediatric nurse? But it didn't matter. He was the cutest idiot she'd ever laid eyes on.

"Okay, cool. That's tight that your mom works late hours; gives us a chance to get in some quality time. What y'all got up in this piece to eat, ma?"

"Same old, same old. Frozen pizza. You want a slice?"

"Yeah, I'm hungry."

"You want something to drink with it?"

"Bet, straight up with a lil' ice."

Todd had a street temperament that Reign found alluring. Every time he called her "ma," every tooth in her mouth would gleam in approval, even the two extra ones in the back. Ma was a term of endearment, like baby or honey, but sweeter. It was so sexy how the word just rolled off his tongue. It was his ghetto way of being affectionate.

"Ma, your mom got any beer or Hennessy in there?"

"Like, alcohol?"

"Yeah."

"You drink beer and stuff?" Reign asked, surprised.

"Here and there."

"I didn't know you drank."

"It relaxes me. Takes the pressure off things, and makes me feel like a boss."

"Well, we don't have any of that. We got some lemon-lime soda."

"Cool. I can mix it."

"Mix what?"

"Some Henny and lemon-lime."

"So, wait a minute. You got some Hennessy with you, now?"

"Don't leave home without it!"

"Dang, boy! How much do you drink?"

"It ain't like that. I told you—only when I want to relax."

"You're only eighteen, Todd. You telling me you need alcohol to relax?"

"Not all the time, but if I did, so what?"

"Ever heard of the phrase *underage drinking*?"

"Come on, ma; it's the twenty-first century. Who waits until they're twenty-one? Just chill and try some wit me."

"I don't know."

"Just a sip. It won't kill you."

"Okay. Maybe just a taste." Reign grabbed a couple of paper cups and the two-liter bottle of lemon-lime soda from the kitchen. There was no way she was allowing Todd to drink out of her mom's glasses. She couldn't believe he was already drinking hard liquor, and carrying the shit with him. It was so crazy. Now, she was actually going to try some, too.

"What's taking you so long?"

"I'm coming! Had to find the paper cups." She sat the soda and cups down in front of Todd on a coffee table. He filled each with a little soda and a lot of Hennessy.

"Try this first and see if it's too strong." Todd held a cup up to Reign's mouth. The taste wasn't as bad as she thought; she actually liked it. The lemon-lime flavor overpowered the alcohol. She thought it would have been the opposite, even though she'd heard somewhere that Hennessy was a smooth liquor. Now, she was able to discern that "smooth" meant you basically couldn't taste the alcohol.

"You cool, Reign?"

"Yeah, I'm good." She was hesitant, but more curious to find out how drinking alcohol would make her feel. She continued to drink.

"Todd, did you bring any DVDs?"

"Two. You wanna pop one in?"

Kayla's words kept replaying in Reign's head. She was right. Todd was nothing but an invitation to temptation. That night, he was rocking a pair of dark-blue True Religion jeans, matching t-shirt, and a pair of navy Jordons. He had a one-carat diamond earring in his left ear, accessorized by a phat watch and platinum link bracelet. He could have been a model on the pages of *GQ*. Reign was really feeling his look and his vibe.

He was always dressed to impress, and seemed to have a lot of cash. He would sometimes splurge and spend some of it on Reign. He had taken her to the mall a couple of times and bought her a pair of tennis shoes, designer jeans, and a silver ring. He had convinced her that a guy only spent money on a girl he really liked.

Reign placed one of the movies Todd had brought into the DVD player, titled *Humping Around.* "What kind of title is this?" Reign asked. "Oh my God, Todd! Is this porn?"

"What's wrong, baby? You act like you've never seen porn."

"I haven't!"

"Nothing to be scared of."

"I'm not scared; it's sinful!"

"We commit sins every day. Why is this different?"

"Yeah … but… but…" Reign was at a loss for words. She was astonished by the images flashing before her. The human body was being displayed in ways that she had never seen before. Something in her spirit challenged whether she should continue to watch. *This is going to mess my head up,* she told herself.

"Ma, chill. Sip your Hen and relax."

The background music in the scenes was dramatic and slow; almost like it was being played in slow motion. A statuesque black woman dominated every scene. She had huge, round butt cheeks that resembled two beach balls. Reign had never seen a woman with a buttocks that size. She wondered if it was real.

The scene opened with the woman lying naked on a beach. A man appeared, running all dramatic and stuff, with no clothes on. *Who runs butt-naked on the damned beach?* His thang was swinging from side to side, hitting his thighs. It was long, thick, and destructive looking. Reign had heard friends at school talk about dudes with big wieners, but it was her first time seeing one with her own eyes. She couldn't even imagine where and how it would fit, inside of anything! Did her body have enough room to hold something like that? It was hard for Reign to assimilate what she was watching.

The man in the scene grabbed the woman around her neck and started to kiss and caress her breasts. He licked and kissed, kissed and licked, for what seemed like hours. Reign's mind started to play tricks on her.

Suddenly, she and Todd had replaced the couple on the beach. Todd was kissing her naked body. Licking and kissing, kissing and licking. It felt so good. Now, it was Reign being grabbed by the neck and French kissed. Todd's tongue tasted so sweet and felt so warm in her mouth. He slowly twirled it around her mouth and all over her face. The tingling feeling between her legs was stronger than it had ever been.

"Ha-ha-ha-ha!" was the sound of Reign bursting into a girlish laughter.

"What's so funny?"

"I don't know—it feels good and tickles at the same time, Todd."

"Tickles?"

"Yes."

"Does it feel good?"

"I guess." The truth was, Reign was beginning to feel strange in ways she had never experienced before. Her lips were numb, her vision was blurred, but Todd still looked so damn good. She could feel his wetness between her legs. She wasn't quite sure what it was, but it made her body pulsate. She became more and more comfortable with Todd's touch. He had a way of just relaxing her, like the Hennessy relaxed him.

His touch escalated to the duty of unbuttoning Reign's shirt, and in less than a second it was lying on the floor. She was down to just her jeans and panties. Todd smoothly removed her bra, without her even realizing. He slowly fondled her nipples and chest with the tip of his tongue. Reign's nipples had become so hard she could no longer feel them. He gratified every inch of her torso, even kissing and licking it at intervals.

She thought the best thing to do would be to return his actions. The girls in her peer circle gossiped that men liked the same thing sexually as women. Todd's shirt was already practically off, so she didn't have to wrestle with it much. Reign kissed his chest and played with his nipples. She could see and feel his body reacting to her touch as he jerked and moaned loudly. She guessed it felt good to him.

"Reign. Ma, stop! You're gonna make me come!"

Reign couldn't believe how easy and pleasurable sex was. It felt incredible. Her body was hot, and she was enjoying every moment of her first experience. She kissed Todd on his stomach, just like the woman on the DVD kissed the man. She must have nailed the technique in one try, because Todd's body jumped every time her lips touched him.

"Slow down, ma. I'm not ready yet; I want to enjoy you some more."

His words stunned her. The thought crossed her mind that Kayla was wrong after all. Sex wasn't just about Todd getting pleasure; Reign was now convinced he wanted her to experience pleasure as well. Being her first time, she wasn't exactly sure of what to do or what gave her the most pleasure. But it all gave her an unbelievable sensation.

When Todd started to slide her jeans off, she couldn't have resisted if she'd wanted. She was caught up in the moment and didn't want to say no … to anything. Her panties were the next thing to go, and Todd's touch felt more intense with every stroke. No wonder everybody in church preached sex was so wrong. Something that felt so good had to be sinful. Finally, she felt what might be Todd's penis trying to enter her.

"Wait, wait, wait!"

"What's wrong, Reign?"

"Do you have a condom?"

"No."

"We can't do it without a condom."

"Why do we a need condom?"

"Because, we need to protect ourselves."

"From what?"

"Pregnancy. Disease," Reign cautioned through her slurred speech.

"Baby, you forgot? I've never had sex, so ain't no diseases to worry about. And I can pull out before I come so you don't get pregnant."

He pulled ferociously at her body, kissing as she spoke. "I don't know, Todd. I still think we need a condom."

"But don't you feel good down there?"

"Yeah."

"You like this?" Todd sucked the inside of her thighs. "Don't spoil this moment for us, baby."

He licked her left nipple, then her right. Her navel. Her hips. For a virgin, he somehow knew all the right things to do. Reign's mind was fuzzy, and she couldn't think straight. The room wouldn't stop spinning. It was like she was on a carousel and the speed had been switched to level ten. But his touch felt so good that she couldn't resist; there was no way she was going to tell him to stop. Maybe it would hurt less without a condom, and she was only making an exception for this one time.

"I don't know if we should, Todd," she tested once again.

"Why?"

"I keep telling you, because we don't have a condom."

"We'll be okay. I wanna feel our bare skin rubbing against each other, and a condom would get in the way."

Before Reign could even say no again, Todd had inserted himself into her. Everyone had said it would hurt the first time, but it didn't. Todd went slowly, and before she knew it, he had thrust a few times ... and it was over. His body was all sweaty, and he was comatose. Reign felt like she could go on, but not without another able body. Todd was lifeless. *I guess that's what people look like when they come.* Reign wondered if the come thing had happened to her, too. Todd looked happy as he slept. She eventually dozed off and awoke to find the DVD clock displaying a time of eleven thirty.

Her head was pounding, vision foggy, and her body racked with panic. "Todd, wake up!" she screamed at him.

"Hmm, hmm, uh ... uh."

"Todd, you have to go! Now!"

"Why? What time is it?"

"It's eleven thirty, and my mom will be home anytime now. You gotta go fa real!"

"Okay. Okay. Let me get my stuff."

Todd hazily collected his clothes while Reign slipped on her shirt, embarrassed for him to see her fully naked. He stood before her naked, with everything showing. He was scratching, rubbing, still kind of hard. While Todd gathered his things and got dressed, Reign began her cleanup of all signs of unauthorized company.

"Did you enjoy yourself, Reign?"

"It was cool."

"Just cool? Why not great?"

"I wish we could have used a condom."

"I told you everything is straight, baby."

"That's easy for you to say."

"For real. You don't have anything to worry about."

"How do you know?"

"I didn't come inside of you."

"How would I know?"

"Come on, ma. I wouldn't do that to you."

"Why?"

"I ain't tryin' to be no baby daddy right now, and I'm feeling you."

"Feeling me?"

"Yeah, I like your style and your energy. Somethin' 'bout you is different."

"Different how, Todd?"

"Tonight it was the booty."

"That's all you wanted?"

"No, but it didn't hurt. You know I like spending time with you. Why don't you go take a shower? It'll help you calm down and get back right," Todd suggested.

"I'll do that when you leave. I feel dirty, my head is spinning, and I'm dizzy like crazy."

"It's probably that Hen messing with you. That shower will help you shake it off. Do that and get some rest," Todd instructed as he leaned in to kiss Reign good-bye.

Reign felt icky and unclean. She didn't want to kiss Todd, and turned her face from him to avoid the kiss.

"We'll talk tomorrow, ma," Todd said as he headed out the front door.

"Okay. Bye, Todd."

"Stay sexy."

Reign ran to the shower, set the water as hot as she could take it, and jumped in. She bathed every inch of her body, but still felt impure afterwards. She put on her pajamas and took two Tylenol for her splitting headache. Minutes after jumping into bed, she heard the key turning in the lock of the front door. She knew it had to be her mother. She breathed a deep sigh of relief that she was already tucked in, and wouldn't need an excuse for why she was up so late on a school night.

She closed her eyes and began to think about Todd. They were angry thoughts, tainted by the realization that she had lost her virginity. She was no longer a virgin, but she knew Todd was not to blame. After all, she had agreed to the act. There was no force involved. In that instance, Reign knew she had made a very adult choice that no amount of anger or fear could change.

CHAPTER 8

Lunch with Lust

"So, today is the day you go to lunch with the elusive Mr. Orray, huh?"

"Yes, Reagan. I guess you could say I'm mildly excited about it. At the very least, I can fill an hour in the middle of my day with some good eatin'."

"That's the wrong attitude, Kennedy; he might be all right."

"Of course, it's a possibility, but I'm not hanging my hat on it. The brutha is too smooth and too fine not to have some bones in his closet."

"Well, whatever he is or ain't, you can only blame yourself, because that's all you ever attract ... smooth and fine."

"Yep, and it's gotten me all the way to absolutely ... nowhere!"

"True, but I think a lot of that has to do with you, Kennedy. When Ryan and I got married, I was ready to juggle a husband and a career. You, on the other hand, are afraid of that level of commitment."

"That's not true! I just don't like to deal with a whole lot of crap. I don't have time for games, Reagan. I've been playing games since high school, when I asked Jerome to check a YES or NO box if he wanted to be my boyfriend. In those days, everything seemed so harmless. My only care was whether a boy was cute or popular. At that age, a boy being saved, having a car, kids, or steady job, wasn't even a factor. But grown-folk dating is the real world. It's way too complicated."

"Just take a deep breath and stay in the positive, girlfriend. What time is your date?"

"One."

"Don't you think you better get going?"

"He probably borrowed his boy's car to get to the restaurant, is jobless, has a wife, or maybe even six kids with six baby mommas."

"Jesus of Nazareth, girl! Will you just give the man a chance? He only asked you out to lunch, not to bear him identical quintuplets."

Here we go again, displayed on a banner in Kennedy's head. Another man. Another date. Another meal laden with fifty million who, what, why, and when questions. Like, what do you do in your spare time? What spare time? It was a luxury Kennedy never had. Dating had become a ritualistic mating dance that always ended with a melancholy soundtrack playing in her head. Kennedy was sick of the lunch, dinner, dancing, or a movie dating routine.

Sometimes it took her more than one round in front of the dating firing squad to get a real feel for a guy. Some men were really good at playing "the part" on the first couple of dates. But, the minute he'd get the impression Kennedy wanted to take it to the next level, he'd start tripping. 'We ain't in no relationship. You can't dictate what I do or where I go. I'm still trying to find myself.' And the worst part would always be when a busta would throw out the big joker card of excuses, also known as, projecting. Projecting emotions was a playa's way of flipping the script. "You've changed. What happened to the old you? We don't click like we used to." But it was all baseless BS. The same habits that were cool for a woman to do in the beginning of dating would all of a sudden become unacceptable. Kennedy had witnessed a sea of fine men morph into fine idiots.

I wish God would just drop a man into my lap and make it obvious that he's the one, Kennedy thought. *Lord, please send me what I need, and a little bit of what I want*, she prayed as she left Crimson on her way to Rosario's.

"Hi. Reservation for two, Johnson, one o'clock."

"Ms. Johnson, the other half of your party hasn't arrived yet. Would you like to wait at the bar or be seated?"

"I'll have a seat, thank you." Kennedy couldn't believe she'd beat Orray there. Maybe being early was a good sign. *Things might be all right after all*, she started to coach herself through the moment. *You're doing it again, Kennedy… stop trying to make something out of nothing. This is just a first date; nothing more.* She decided to occupy the time by being productive and working on her agenda for an afternoon meeting. She ordered a glass of Prosecco and pulled out her iPad. Her cell phone rang before she could press the power button.

"Hello."

"What's up, Kennedy?"

"Nothing, Rick. How are things in your world?"

"Can't complain. What happened to you the other night? I was told you didn't pick up the tickets I left for you at Will Call.

"I'm so sorry. I should have called to explain. I got stuck at work."

"Excuses."

"No, for real, Rick. I had to take care of some pressing stuff at Crimson."

"It's cool. I understand if you didn't wanna see a brutha run up and down the hardwood. Anyway, did I catch you at a bad time?"

"Not really, I'm just waiting on this guy I met the other night. We're supposed to be having lunch."

"Oh, all right, ummm … well … I won't hold you then. I was just checking in to see what happened."

"I know you probably had some side chick there on standby."

"I might have, but you know, you're my girl, and you always come first. Our friendship is tighter than any side chick."

"Okay, silver-tongued man. I'll holler at you later."

Kennedy had a perfect view of the restaurant's main entrance. She was anxious to check out Orray's persona before he made it to the table. *He'll probably be wearing some too-tight, Kanye West tapered jeans, or dress pants with a floral pattern and a fitted short-sleeve shirt*, she teased in her head.

She had resolved that most fine men just didn't know how to dress, but the mediocre-looking ones usually stepped out like they'd been styled for a Bloomingdale's catalogue. For Kennedy, a man dressing to the nines was more than adequate compensation for his lack in the looks department.

Kennedy also gave major points to men with a tight shoe game. Footwear was imperative—a brutha in a nice pair of kicks was always guaranteed a glance, if not a stare. Scuffed-up or run-over shoes earned enough demerits for immediate detention. A shiny pair of leather dress shoes or spotless, white sneakers was a huge turn-on.

Kennedy glanced at her watch. It was twelve fifty-five. *Okay, he has until ten after, and I'm out.* It was a grace protocol she'd picked up in college. If a professor didn't show for a class by ten minutes after the start time, class was cancelled. Orray, too, would be cancelled after ten minutes, and there would be no second chance. *How dare he keep me waiting? I've got too much to do to wait on a man. Wait on a man? Never.*

Before another string of thoughts could enter her mind, she looked up to find Orray walking toward her table. She knew a man who looked as good as he did in workout clothes had mega potential, but she never imaged it could get as good as what she was looking at.

Her eyes went straight to his feet and noticed a pair of polished, black, square-toe Kenneth Coles. His dress slacks were perfectly tailored; not too tight; not too long. The outer seams of his pants outlined his protruding thigh muscles. His dress shirt was creased in all the right places and fell evenly across his broad shoulders and pecs.

His mustache and beard were nicely trimmed and framed his mouth of beautiful, mother-of-pearl-white teeth. Making a beeline to Kennedy he smiled from ear to ear, emphasizing the nickel-sized dimples in his cheeks. The one-carat diamond studs in his ears beamed like headlights, and the waves in his hair were already giving Kennedy ocean sickness. He was a stunner!

"Hello, Ms. Johnson."

"Hi, Orray. You had exactly ten more minutes before I left."

"Oh, you got time limits for dates?"

"I sure do. I'm a busy woman, and I don't have time to wait… or waste."

"And I'm a busy man—that's why I'm here on time. It's one o' clock, right?"

Kennedy's heart was racing like an Olympic sprinter. His looks were giving her heart palpitations. He had a face and savoir faire that would rival any mega movie star. He could run with the best of 'em: Morris Chestnut in *Best Man*, Denzel in *Training Day*, or Dwayne Wade (on and off the court). *Boy, Satan, you are one bad mutha, and you know exactly how to get my goose. Lord, help me get my head right. Remove the lust from my flesh. Help me focus on the qualities that are eternal, long-lasting, and life-fulfilling*, Kennedy prayed.

The question of his occupation reentered her mind, because any man that well-groomed had to have a little paper stored up somewhere. But asking too soon might earn her a gold digger label.

"I'm glad you stayed, and I have to admit, you're a very attractive woman, Kennedy."

"Thank you, you're not so bad yourself."

"Kennedy, you know, I hate the game of twenty-one questions, so let's cut to the chase. What do you wanna know about me?"

"What do you wanna confess?"

"Anything you want to ask."

"Kids?" Kennedy initiated with the speed and vigor of a gameshow host.

"No. You?"

"No."

"Wifey?" Kennedy jabbed.

"No. Husband?" Orray shot back.

"No. Umm, girlfriend?"

"No. Boyfriend?"

"No. What about an out-of-town lover, Orray?"

"No. Are you a lesbian, Kennedy?" Orray asked playfully.

"Hell no. You're not gay, are you?"

"I can assure you, Kennedy. I exclusively prefer the company of a woman."

Their speed round of twenty-one questions ended after less than a dozen queries. And, even though she'd been given permission, Kennedy still opted not to ask questions about his work. She decided it would only lead to Orray thinking that money was her number one priority. It was in her top five, but he didn't need to know that.

A waiter approaching their table was a perfect timeout. "You folks ready to order?"

"Ladies first," Orray offered.

"Yes, I'll have the chicken and red pepper linguini."

"And I'll try that lunch prime rib," Orray followed.

"Would you like another glass of wine, ma'am?"

"Not right now, thank you," Kennedy responded, quickly returning full attention to her date.

"Orray Philips, are you still working out at the gym? I haven't seen you lately."

"No, I don't work out there. The day I met you was the one and only time I've been there. I happened to be on that side of town, and stopped in to check out the facility. I actually work out at another gym downtown."

"Okay, interesting. By the way, how was your business trip?"

"It was productive. My job involves quite a bit of seasonal travel."

It was Kennedy's perfect opportunity to ask, "What do you do?" But the words wouldn't leave her tongue. She just couldn't ask, and he seemed conspicuously comfortable not volunteering additional information. Asking about professions or talking about salaries were just not first-date questions, and Kennedy was a master at holding to her two-date wait rule. No ultra-serious or "qualifying" questions before the third date.

Everything about Orray's presence matched that of a businessman, but what type? Maybe he just looked the part, but underneath it all was as broke as a guitar string. The last thing Kennedy needed was a man who couldn't afford to take care of himself.

She glanced down at Orray's diamond-studded Rolex watch, noticing is was three thirty—the time had flown. What seemed like an hour had actually been two and a half.

"Orray, I've really enjoyed myself this afternoon, and I hate to cut it off, but I have a four o' clock meeting across town with some vendors for Crimson."

"So soon? Maybe we can do a sequel later in the week?"

"I wouldn't mind that at all." Kennedy was slightly embarrassed over how she'd flirted with Orray throughout lunch. She had batted her eyes, twirled her hair, tilted her head, and did everything possible to let him know she was feeling him.

"How about dinner Friday or Sunday? I'm leaving town again on Saturday, but I'll be back Sunday morning," Orray shared. "So, if you want to get together on Sunday, I'm free any time after church."

Are my ears deceiving me, or did this brutha just say he was going to church on Sunday? I don't believe it. He's saved? Or is he going to a mosque, synagogue, or Kingdom Hall?

"Oh, where do you go to church?"

"I haven't been in Cleveland too long, so I've just been visiting different ones until I find a church home, but I like Mt. Moriah."

Lord, he's been to The Mount? Kennedy had attended Mt. Moriah and knew it was a Bible-based church that believed in Jesus Christ and the Holy Trinity. *Yes, Lord, you've dropped him in my lap. Now, let's see if I can hold onto him.* The afternoon had equipped Kennedy with more than enough details, and she felt it best not to ask more questions.

"Do you go to church, Kennedy?"

"Yes, I'm a member of Western Bethany."

"Oh, that's the big church on 90th Street."

"Yep, I was born and raised in that neighborhood."

"I know I'm putting myself out there asking you this question … but, umm … only because we're on the topic … do you mind if I ask if you've accepted Jesus Christ as your Lord and personal Savior?"

Okay, Jesus! You 'bout to give me a stroke! I'm feeling weak and lightheaded. This man was really sent by you, wasn't he? A black man curious about my salvation could only be your doing! "Yes, Orray, I have. What about you?"

"I have, and I never thought I would ask someone about salvation on a first date. It's funny how God works things out when you ask that his will be done. I've been praying he'd send me a friend I could laugh and have fun with; someone whose company I'd enjoy with no pretense. Today, you've given me the impression that someone could be you, Kennedy."

This man was more than Kennedy had bargained for, and it wasn't like he was making moves to get in her panties or take her home. He didn't even appear to be lusting. He seamlessly presented himself as a man who went to church, believed in Jesus Christ, dressed immaculately, and looked like a Nubian god. As if that didn't suffice, he even had the nerve to care about the soul of the woman sitting across from him.

"Orray, I can't remember the last time I met a man of your caliber. Why aren't you in a relationship?"

"I could ask you the same question, Kennedy. And you'd probably give me an answer equal to what I'm about to tell you—because God hasn't said so."

"Exactly. Men ask me that all the time. Unfortunately, it's not that simple. Being attractive doesn't bump you to the top of the I'm Taken list. The few bruthas I had chemistry with or thought had possibility for longevity, God removed from my life. Losing what I thought had promise to become something meaningful cut deep. But, I've grown to understand that God always intervenes to make room for something better."

"I feel you on that. I've felt like some possible Mrs. material has slipped through my fingers, but every last one was with me for the wrong reasons. A few just viewed me as a showpiece."

"Showpiece? Please."

"I'm dead serious, Kennedy. If you think women are only used for arm candy, think again. Men get used as display case trophies all the time. As if to say, 'Hey, world! Look what I got!'"

"You trippin'. That's the craziest thing I've heard all day, Orray."

"Crazy or not, it's true, Kennedy. Men and women are different, yet so much alike."

"True, and men are generally all about what they want, when they want it, and who they want it with."

"So are women."

"No, in most situations, women are usually the ones who give in and lower their standards. We're always the ones to compromise. Men don't compromise often, but they're quick to do what's convenient or feels right in the moment."

"And women don't?"

"Orray, when was the last time you put the moves on a woman to get her to bend and she eventually broke?"

"Today. When you saw how good I looked, but you didn't compromise your standards."

"Funny! Orray, reeeally funny. Don't tell me you're arrogant, too."

"Arrogant? Not even in the neighborhood. Confident? Yes."

"You're a pretty cool dude, Mr. Phillips."

"I can't complain about you either, Ms. Johnson."

"This lunch date got better with every passing minute, but I have to go now. Let's do dinner on Sunday after church."

"Bet. I'll look forward to seeing you then. Let me get that for you," Orray offered, standing up to pull out Kennedy's chair as they both proceeded toward the restaurant's door.

CHAPTER 9

Confession

"**H**ey, Kennedy."

"What's up, Amber?"

"Just hitting you up because I didn't see you back at Crimson after lunch."

"I had a meeting at four, some other stuff to do, and decided not to come back. What do you want, Nosy Rosie?"

"Soooo, does he have a job? Girl, what kind of car does he drive? Did you find out where the man lives?"

"Amber, why are you so obsessed with Orray's financial state?"

"Honey, I'm obsessed with anything that could potentially contribute to my financial state. You should be, too"

"You're a maniac."

"Call me whatever you want! Truth is, if a man has all those things, I'm pretty certain he can afford to take care of someone else."

"See, that's how sistas be falling for bustas. We only look on the surface, when the real deal is hiding beneath. Like, when a man has all the trappings, but he's a street pharmacy, driving his baby mama's Benz, and living in his mama's basement."

Both laughed until tears welled in their eyes and Amber asked, "Kennedy, come on now, give me the dets on your lunch with Orray."

"Amber, girl, forget handsome, that man is straight-up beautiful."

"Not beautiful, girl?"

"Yes, beautiful. I had the best time, and we talked for hours. But, I still don't have any idea of what he does for a living. Granted, he was dressed like a businessman, but what does that mean?"

"Absolutely nothing."

"He did say he traveled a lot, but not for long periods of time, and only during certain times of the year."

"Kennedy, why didn't you just freggin ask? Gosh darnit!"

"You and your gosh darnits, Amber. You know the game—if I ask too soon, he'll think I'm pursuing him for the wrong reason. So, since it didn't come up, I let sleeping dogs lie."

"That's so stupid. What if he never mentions it?"

"Then I guess I'll be still wondering on the 32nd of Neverary."

"So, you would actually date this man without knowing what he does?"

"As long as there are no signs of illegal activity, he never asks me for money, and he treats me right—yeah, I would. I'll find out sooner or later, and I bet you anything he's the type who won't tell unless asked."

"Well, since you didn't find out the most important thing, can you at least tell me what he's like?"

"He's very well mannered, considerate, and easygoing."

"You gathered all that from one lunch date?"

"I sure did, Ms. Thang. First of all, he was a complete gentleman, and allowed me to order first. That was a biggie for me. He didn't do the chauvinistic thing and try to order for me. When the waiter came, he simply looked over at me and said, 'Ladies first.' "

"Sexy."

"I know, right? He also made it a point to pull out my chair, and open the door when we left the restaurant."

"I guess chivalry's making a comeback, Kennedy."

"That's not all. He didn't play the twenty-one questions game. He told me he hated the monotony of first-date questions, and opened the door for me to ask whatever I wanted."

"And you didn't ask about his j-o-b? Girl, bye!"

"No! How many times do I have to tell you, I couldn't bring it up in our initial conversation? You must want me to be mislabeled."

"You're an idiot. Why would I want that?"

"Listen, I've never met a man like Orray, ever. I just wanted to be on my best behavior. We had such a good time that we scheduled our next date for this Sunday, *after church*."

"Church?"

"Yes. I may have not had the 'what do you do?' conversation, but I managed to get in all of my spirituality inquiries."

"Lexi will be glad to know that."

"But that's not even the real dish. The real tea is that he initiated the discussion."

"A black man who goes to church without a woman pulling out her whip? Shocker."

"That's an understatement, Amber."

"Wait! What time is it?" Amber asked, sounding fearful that she'd lost track of time.

"Almost six. Why? Is Reign seeing you for tutoring tonight?"

"She's supposed to, but she's missed her last couple of sessions. Not sure what's up with her."

"What do you mean?"

"I don't know. She's been acting strange lately."

"Strange how?" Kennedy dug.

"Just usually preoccupied."

"She's probably having some struggles adjusting to adolescence, like most teenagers."

"Maybe. Whatever it is, she's noticeably different. Typically, she'll call on Saturdays and ask if we can do our weekend run to the movies or mall."

"She didn't call last Saturday?"

"Not until late, and only to say she was too tired to do anything. She said she'd been at the mall all day with Kayla."

"That could be true—it's not uncommon for teenagers to spend the whole day hanging at the mall. It's normal for kids to want to hang around their peers more than adults. Kayla adores you, Amber, but she's still a kid."

"Speak of the devil, I mean the little darling, that sounds like my doorbell, Kennedy. Must be Reign. I'll hollatcha later."

* * *

"Hi, Ms. Amber," Reign greeted her softly.

"Hey, Reign. I'm glad you decided to show tonight."

"Aww, come on, Ms. Amber. I've just been busy lately with school, the recital, and Kayla."

"It's okay, baby. I'm only kidding; come on in."

"Thanks, Ms. Amber. Of all people, I knew you would understand."

"Well, I understand school should be your first priority, not the mall, looking at boys, and all the other mess that has you distracted."

"What's wrong with looking at boys? I like boys!"

"Okay, little girl, you better ice those raging hormones. Lock in, let's get started with your math first."

"Good, math is kicking my butt, and I've got a big test next week."

"How about I order pizza? We can study while we wait on it."

"Sounds good."

"What trouble are you having with math?"

"I just don't understand it."

"What don't you understand?"

"Everything: geometry, algebra, formulas—it's all Chinese to me."

"Are you reading your lessons before class, doing homework and the practice problems?"

"No."

"Child, how do you expect to understand if you don't study and practice?"

"Good point."

"Okay, open your book. I want to start with principles and geometry terms, first. Do you understand point, line, line segment, ray, angle, and triangle?"

"What's the difference?"

"You read it, Reign, and tell me." Reign paused for a moment to read the lesson. After a few minutes Amber asked, "Okay, what's the difference between a line and a line segment?"

"A line goes to infinity, and a line segment has a beginning and ending point."

"Correct. Can you name the angles?"

"Angle AED and angle DEA," Reign answered with hesitation.

"Yes! I think you got this part."

"Thanks, Ms. Amber."

"If you really want to get this down, you have to read and practice religiously. Let's try a few more." Reign continued working as Amber jumped up at the sound of her doorbell chiming.

"That must be the pizza. Reign, will you get the door while I go grab my wallet?"

"Yes, I can't wait to eat. I'm so hungry. I feel like I haven't eaten in days."

"You're always hungry, little girl," Amber said, handing a twenty-dollar bill to the pizza delivery driver through a barely opened front door. "That's nothing unusual for you. By the way, how's your mom?"

"She's fine, just working all the time. Her new job is keeping her busy."

"Is she gone most evenings?"

"Yep, and being an only child, I get really lonely."

"Well, your mother is doing the best she can as a single parent."

"Oh, I know. She's a good mom. I just wish she didn't work so much."

"Where's Kayla tonight?"

"She had to dance at the City Annual Gospel Fest."

"Why didn't you go?"

"Because I needed tutoring."

"Reign, you and Kayla are inseparable; you support each other in everything. Come on now—what's the real reason you didn't go?"

"I just didn't feel like it. Plus, I needed help with my math."

"Reign, you and I both know that's not the real reason. You must've forgot I was once sixteen, too."

"Really?"

"Umm … yeah … duh."

"Kayla and I have just been arguing a lot lately, so sometimes I need a break from that girl."

"What are you arguing about?"

"Todd."

"Who's Todd, and what does he have to do with anything?"

"You remember Todd. My boyfriend!"

"Boyfriend? No, I've never heard you mention the name Todd."

"Yes you have. Remember, he was at Crimson one day, and I introduced you."

"Oh, that little sexy young thing who had on the Timbs with his baseball cap covering half his face?"

"Yep, that's him."

"Okay, he's a little cutie."

"Ms. Amber, you not checking for my man, are you?"

"Reign, I'd run rings around you and your man."

"You think?"

"I don't think—I know. There's nothing a young boy can do for me. He doesn't even have a real job. Working at the mall is fine when you're under twenty, but I need a man with benefits and a 401(k)."

"That's what I'm talking about, Ms. Amber, a man with some money."

"Okay, you've been listening to my talk track a little too much. Simmer down, young lady. Anyway, what does Todd have to do with your and Kayla's relationship?"

"I don't know. She's just been trippin'."

"About what? Does she have a crush on him or something?"

"No, far from it. She thinks he's full of it."

"And what do you think?"

"I think he's hot. We have fun together."

"What's wrong with having fun?" Amber pressed for understanding.

"Nothing, but Kayla says he's tempting me."

"What gives her that idea?"

"Ms. Amber, if I tell you, you promise not tell my mom or anyone else?"

"Reign, stop. Don't tell me. Please don't say what I think you're going to."

"I'm not a virgin anymore, Ms. Amber."

"What? How did that happen?"

"How do you think?"

"You had sex?"

"Yes, with Todd."

"You had sex with Todd. What? Really?"

"Breathe, Ms. Amber. Please, breathe."

"I can't… go get me some water. Oh, not sex! Lord, not sex."

"Ms. Amber, it's okay. It's not the end of the world. I'm still a good person."

"It hurts—I can't. It hurts. My heart hurts, Reign. You're too young for sex! You don't even know where it's supposed to go, or what to do with it. Jesus, Jesus, Jesus! Lord, have mercy. Have mercy on this poor child's soul!"

"I lost my virginity to Todd, but he was a virgin, too."

"And you told Kayla?"

"Yeah, and now she's always trying to lecture me about using protection, not doing it anymore, and going to the clinic to get checked out."

"She's right, Reign! I don't blame her. That's what friends are for. Are you listening to her?"

"Yes, I listen, but not to her lectures."

"Maybe you should. How many times did you guys do it?"

"Once."

"Did you use protection?"

"No."

"What the hell do you mean, no?"

"No. We were careful. He pulled out."

"Reign, are you kidding me? Don't tell me you're not using protection! A month ago you were coming to school with milk from your cereal around your top lip! Now you telling me that you're all good because some boy pulled out of you? You don't know a damn thing about pulling out!"

"All I know is he's the first person I've had sex with, and we both wanted to see what it felt like without him having anything on."

"I swear, girl, you're about to give me a heart attack!"

"Ms. Amber, I feel so special when I'm with him. He tells me he loves me all the time. He pays me so much attention, and the time we had sex felt so good. I got all these tingling feelings and stuff. My legs throbbed, my heart was beating out of my chest, and I couldn't resist him. We made love. It was like magic, until he feel asleep."

"You made love? Reign, what you made was lust!"

"No, it wasn't; it was love."

"Reign, you are too young to even understand what love is and what it truly feels like. Love is more than sex. What you felt was your body releasing chemicals and hormones. Love is so much deeper than sex."

"Well, Todd says he loves me."

"Most men will say they love you, if it'll get your pants down to your ankles."

"But he gives me all the attention in the world. Whenever I tell him my mom is working late, he makes it a point to come over."

"Reign, he does that because he knows he can have sex with you while she's not there. Sweetheart, love between a boy and a girl is conditional—it changes like the weather. I wish you had talked to me, your mom, Kennedy, or anybody before doing this. It's a major step in your life, and you can never go back. Sex changes everything about you. It fast-forwards your emotions and exposes you to physical desires you may not be ready for. Sex is very emotional for females; it plays games with your mind. How could you possibly be prepared to deal with this at sixteen?"

"Ms. Amber, please don't worry about me. I told you, we only did it one time, and I really was ready."

"No, you weren't, Reign!"

"I was. For real!"

"No, you weren't! Had you truly been ready you would've used a condom."

"Being ready doesn't mean using a condom."

"Actually, it does, Reign! Being ready means you at least understand the pros and cons of sex. Being ready has everything to do with being able to control your body's response to touch. Being ready is more than reacting to tingling sensations between your legs or a boy whispering I love you in your ear. Reign, you weren't and still aren't ready for sex."

"Well, it's too late to go back now."

"It is, but it's not too late to be responsible."

"Responsible how?"

"Learning the importance and necessity of using protection. You have got to use a condom. Too many things can happen without protection. You can get pregnant, or even worse, contract an incurable sexually transmitted disease, like AIDS."

"I told you, Todd said he was a virgin, too. He's only had sex with me."

"And you believe him? How old is Todd?"

"I do. He's eighteen."

"Hot between the legs, but not sleeping around with anyone else. Come on, Reign; you're young, but you're a lot smarter than you are acting."

"I'm not acting. I believe Todd."

"I don't. Most men think with their penises, so it's a woman's duty to protect herself in every situation. Have you had sex with him again?"

"No, not yet."

"Well, let me tell you what you are going to do, if it ever happens again—use protection! And I don't want to hear your backtalk or debate. Do I make myself clear?"

"Yes, ma'am."

"It's only for your benefit. How are you protecting yourself from pregnancy?"

"I told you, he pulls out."

"That's not the answer, sweetheart. Did you know a man releases a fluid before he ejaculates that can also get you pregnant? So, with all that pulling out, you can still get pregnant, Reign."

"Yeah, but he pulled out the second he felt it coming."

"Either you're not listening or you don't understand what I'm telling you. That pulling out crap is no guarantee you won't get pregnant. Besides, it only takes one time to get pregnant. What happens the day he doesn't pull out in time? Don't answer that! Here, take these," Amber said, reaching into a nearby dresser drawer, grabbing a box of condoms, and handing them to Reign.

"These are condoms?"

"Yes! Use them, Reign. I mean it!"

CHAPTER 10

It's Ya Burfday

"I swear this party snuck up on me. I can't believe it's been three months since we started the planning."

"It's crazy. Thanks for coming early to help me set up, Kennedy. I couldn't have pulled this off without your and Amber's help," said Reagan.

"I'm glad to be here. It's hard to believe Lexi is thirty! I'm so excited to celebrate with her tonight, but the best part is knowing I'll have a date in tow."

"This one could be the one, Ken."

"Pump your breaks, Reagan. It's way too early to tell."

"I beg to differ. That's the beauty of male-female relationships; even when we don't know what we need, we know what we want, and when we find someone who's willing to satisfy it. But, as women, we're just too afraid to admit it. We know off the bat when a man's worth keeping around, and men have the same radar. Ryan was no different. For about six months we did the no-title thing, insisting we were just friends. He would always tell me he didn't want a relationship, but he did every-thing with me a man does with his girlfriend. We went to each other's family parties, work outings, and saw each other every other night. We even had a set date night. We had all the actions that represented two people being in a relationship, but no titles. I can't lie and say it wasn't difficult on me, because sometimes it was hell, just thinking how badly I could get hurt. And I was getting so much bad relationship advice from girlfriends. 'If a man tells you he doesn't want a relationship, you're a fool if you don't believe him.' I knew Ryan cared about me, but that was never the question. I just didn't know if he'd ever be ready to fully commit. I had to make the tough decision of whether I should wait and risk being hurt, or move on. In the end, I realized finding love is one of the biggest risks you'll ever take in life, and no matter how hard you try, there's always the chance of being hurt."

"I don't know if we share the same process though, Reagan. I'm not one to put myself out there like that, allowing a man to determine the status of our relationship. How's that fair to me?"

"It's not, and unfortunately, that's all people looking from the outside in tend to evaluate—fairness."

"Well, yeah. Do you not understand why? It's selfish for a man to give a woman full girlfriend privileges without a title or commitment. It's dangerous, and leaves the door open for another woman to come in and steal all you've invested."

"I don't think it has anything to do with a man wanting to keep his options open, Kennedy. Some men just don't jump into relationships or assume titles easily because of past fears and experiences. And then you have those who shy away because they're trying to get themselves tight, professionally. Some, just authentically believe in taking it slow."

"Slow? Please, Reagan. How can a man spend the amount of time with a woman that Ryan spent with you and still claim to not want a relationship? Any troll making that claim is just being slick and weighing his options. It's all summed up in the title of that book that came out a few years ago, *He's Just Not that into You*."

"I can't agree with that, Kennedy. Think about my situation. It was almost two years before Ryan said he wanted to commit to me, but he never dated another woman during the time he was unclear."

"You mean, he never dated another woman that you knew of."

"Okay, fine, that I knew of; but what's your point? A man can still date on the side unbeknownst to you, regardless of commitment. As I said before, love is the risk of a lifetime. Now don't get me wrong—there are telltale signs when a man is just not that into you, but most won't invest the kind of time Ryan did if they're not interested. You've got to inspect a man's reasoning behind his decisions. As women, we'll always have that sixth sense to help us discern when something doesn't pass the smell test."

"And that's exactly what I'm doing with Orray—leaning to my own discernment. So far, things are going great. He's the total opposite of every man I've ever dated. He's patient, kind, supportive, and I can never forget to include—fine as all get out. We talk first thing every morning and last thing each night, even when he travels. Our conversation has grown, too. He's started asking about my day, work schedule, how things are going at Crimson, and even the kids. He has a way of making me feel like he actually cares about what's going on in my life. We talk about politics, religion, and the likes of people."

"Kennedy, what the heck are the 'likes of people'?"

"Things people have the choice to change—like their shoes, clothes, hair, your fat butt . . ."

"Oh, so y'all hatin' on my fatty?"

"Not specifically, but now that you've mentioned it, your rear end probably wouldn't be a boring topic of discussion."

"I tell you what! I'll take care of my fat butt when I'm good and ready. You and Orray need to worry about yourselves."

"I know, because you're fappy. Right, Reagan?"

"Fappy?"

"Fat and happy!" Kennedy blurted out, laughing hysterically.

"Whatever! How 'bout I'm fappily married and committed. Now, put that in your fappy pipe and smoke it!"

"Reagan, seriously, I'm not trying to ride you about the weight thing, but we're all getting older and need to focus on health. It wouldn't hurt if you lost a pound or two ... or twenty."

"Kennedy, don't start with me today. I'm not in the mood."

"Okay, fappy, I'll drop it. Let's talk about Orray some more."

"As long as you're happy with him, I'm thrilled. I love the brutha, especially knowing he doesn't mind going up in the Lord's house. My mouth dropped when Alexis told me he was a churchgoing man. You sure that brutha ain't married, Ken?"

"I don't think he is."

"He does travel a lot; maybe he's got a wife in Dallas. Oh, that could be the next big reality show hit, *Housewives of Dallas*, and the show could be centered on Orray's double life. Juicy, huh?"

"Reagan, does your mouth have a power switch? I really feel like turning you off right about now."

"You know I'm only kidding. Anyone who talks to you on the phone the length of time he does when he travels can't be married. He'd be one tired soul, spending hours on the phone with you, then having to repeat the script on the home front. He'd be up all night. After about three or four days of that kind of rigorous pimpin', he'd be like the walking dead."

"Reagan, you ain't got a spoonful of sense."

"I'm just saying. Oh, I forgot to ask, what church does he go to?"

"He's been attending Mt. Moriah since moving from Dallas. He's visited my church a couple of times, too."

"Did he like it?"

"He said it was cool. Right now, we're doing the rotation thing. One week at Moriah, the next at mine."

"You still have no idea what he does for a living?"

"It's irrelevant right now."

"For who?"

"For me."

"Kennedy, I can't believe you've talked around such a focal part of a person's life."

"It just hasn't been the right time, Reagan."

"What's the right time, Kennedy? You just said he asks all the time about your work, Crimson, and the kids; so I know his job has had to come up too, in those conversations."

"Actually, it hasn't, Reagan."

"When he asks about Crimson, why can't you just squeeze it in then?"

"Because; I don't want him to think I'm counting his money and trying to be all up in his pockets."

"So, you'd rather him think of you as a fool than a gold digger. He's gotta know you're purposely avoiding the subject."

"Probably. Maybe that's why he never discusses his job, and he's vague when he talks about work-related travel. He'll say something like, 'I'll only be gone overnight, but you can reach me on my cell. Call me anytime. I'm always wanting to hear a woman's voice, traveling with so many dudes.' Now that I think about, when he talks about work, his dialogue is slightly encrypted."

"And you just sit there like a dummy, and not call him on it. Kennedy Johnson, I'm praying for you."

"Look, I'm going to ask him tonight, okay?"

"You'd better. Has the celibacy thing come up yet?"

"It has."

"And?"

"And what, Reagan?"

"How does he feel about your vow of celibacy? Has he been pressuring you?"

"Reagan, you sound like a teenager at the height of puberty! 'Did you do it yet? How was it? Did it hurt?' "

"I'm curious. You don't find too many men who stick around, knowing a woman's practicing celibacy."

"That's because they're only about the booty. Orray's a different cut of man."

"Whatever, Kennedy. It all just sounds like a bunch of excuses to me. Chil', y'all ain't really even past first base if you scared to ask the man where he works."

"We're close enough for him to know he ain't getting no nookie, and for me to know he doesn't have a problem with it."

"I'm done, girl! Bye, Felicia."

"It's not a big deal, Reagan. I told him I've been celibate for a couple of years."

"Did he ask why?"

"Yes, and I told him I was trying to grow spiritually, but sex was hampering the process. Plus, I work with teenagers. How can I preach abstinence if I'm doing the deed? That's hypocritical."

"Not being celibate doesn't mean you can't advise kid's on doing what's right. Even if you're doing wrong."

"Yeah, but I'm not comfortable telling kids something is wrong when I'm doing it."

"Remember, our mamas used to drill in us, 'do as I say, not as I do.' "

"That doesn't work for me. I'm trying to be a role model to our kids. Anyway, I got tired of sleeping with every man I was semi-attracted to."

"So you were basically tired of hoeing is whatcha sayin'?"

"If that's what you wanna call it, fappy."

"I'm sorry," Reagan said through a heavy chuckle. "I just couldn't resist, Kennedy. But on a serious tip, I very much respect your decision. I've always wished Ryan and I had waited until we were married. But the sex was so legit I got caught up, and look what happened."

"You got the prize; that's what happened. Hopefully, Orray's being truthful that he's not bothered by my celibacy. If he is, I'll have to keep it moving. For right now, all I ask is he continues to respect my decision."

"I like that you're being opened-minded and staying as emotionally free as you were the day he asked for your number."

"Men will be men, Reagan. I can only give Orray credit for where we are now. Tomorrow remains to be seen. Anyway, on another topic, the Crimson kids celebrated Lexi earlier today with a cake and ice cream party, now I'm super-psyched for the big adult shindig tonight."

"Oh my goodness, Kennedy, it's almost seven. The party starts at eight. We've got just enough time to get showered and changed."

Orray and Kennedy had decided it would be more convenient to meet up at the party. It would be his first time meeting Kennedy's inner circle, and anticipating everyone's reaction made Kennedy a little anxious. She almost felt like she was taking him home to meet her parents. The girls exuded a parental-like cynicism where it concerned the guys she dated, though none were more critical than Kennedy herself. If Orray met her approval, meeting Amber, Lexi, and Reagan would be a piece of cake.

* * *

Inside the party, the music was blasting; Amber had hired one of her exes to deejay. Lexi was scheduled to arrive at any moment. Amber, Reagan, and Ryan were sitting at a table, drinking and chatting. Orray had called to say he was en route, and Kennedy was fulfilling her hostess with the mostest role, greeting every guest.

When Lexi and Ray finally arrived, the crowd cheered a birthday song welcome to Lexi. She looked youthfully radiant. In fact, her thirtieth glow was more like a twentieth-something glow or even sweeter—a pregnancy radiance! Lexi had recently found out her ferocious appetite was a result of her being nearly four months pregnant.

"Lexi, you look beautiful, sweetheart."

"Thanks, Kennedy!"

"Hey, Ray. How are you?"

"Good, Kennedy. I can't wait to meet your new friend. Lexi has told me all about him. Is this one a keeper?"

"Oh, God, Lexi loves to flap those loose lips of hers. I hope so, Ray; I really hope so." Kennedy felt a foot tall being questioned about her dating status by Ray. Processing that her friend's husband was keeping score of her dating woes made her feel like a charity case.

As she turned to walk toward Amber and Reagan's table in embarrassment, a deep voice whispered, "You have got to be the baddest woman in here."

She whipped around to discover Orray, dressed to his usual standard of perfection. "Hey, Orray," she said flirtatiously, feeling faint. "You're looking rather dapper yourself." *Kennedy Johnson, that was so corny*, she thought. But in the moment, it was all she could think to say. She was flabbergasted by how good he looked.

"Kennedy, are you all right? Did I startle you?"

"Oh, no, no, no. I'm fine. Just …umm…admiring your suit and tie, that's all."

"There you go again, trying to make me blush."

"Follow me," Kennedy ordered, whisking him off to the head table. "I want to introduce you to my friends. Orray, meet my besties: Amber, Alexis, and Reagan."

"Nice to meet you, ladies."

"Oh, and this is Ray, Alexis's husband … and Ryan, Reagan's husband."

"Orray Philips? Orray of the Cleveland Cavs?" Ray asked. "Hey, man. What's going on?"

A hush fell over the table. Kennedy's shoulders dropped; she looked as if she would pass out. Before she could react to learning that she was dating yet another NBA player, Orray spoke, "Nice to meet you, man. Are you a Cavs fan?"

"Am I?" Ray responded. "Man, you have been on point all season. You're averaging like eighteen points and twelve rebounds a game," Ray bragged. "You're the man!"

Kennedy's vocal cords managed to squeak out a single question, "Orray Philips of the Cleveland Cavs, how come nobody told me?"

Amber blurted out, "Maybe if you'd asked Orray directly, you would've known!"

"I can't believe you play in the NBA."

"Are you upset, Kennedy?"

"I am." Kennedy thought to herself, *now what?*

"Excuse us for a minute, ladies," Orray said, turning his attention away from the table and toward Kennedy. "Kennedy, let's take a walk." Once they were out of earshot, he said, "What's the matter?"

"You're a professional athlete?"

"I am. And?"

"And that makes you incapable of commitment, incapable of being in a relationship, and incapable of monogamy. You're basically a dog!"

"Wait a minute, Kennedy. Slow down."

"I trusted you. I was doing my best to give you a chance; now this!"

"Now what? Kennedy, you didn't know I played ball because you didn't ask. I peeped your game from go. I knew it would only be a matter of time before you asked, but you didn't want to seem desperate or like an opportunist. Right?"

"So why didn't you just tell me then?"

"You're right; I should've. I was afraid you'd stereotype me, just like you're doing now. I am a professional athlete, but my job doesn't dictate anything about my character. Kennedy, open your eyes. Not all professional ballers are dogs."

"That explains all your out-of-town, one-day trips."

"Correct. I was traded to the Cavaliers this season, and I liked the fact that I could maintain a low profile here. That's why I enjoy going places where people won't recognize me ... like church. Why do you think I make a beeline for the front door right after the sermon is over? I was glad when you didn't ask me about my profession, Kennedy. I wanted you to get to know me for who I really am, not for being a famous basketball player. And there's something else I wanna come clean about; I know Rick. He told me all about you. He said you were very sweet and like a sister to him, but he also warned me that your trust had worn thin. I can see he was right."

"Rick? So, that's how you found out where I work?"

"Yep, and had you come to the game that night Rick left tickets at Will Call, you would've found out who I was. I was hoping you'd come so I could tell you everything after that game, but you didn't show. I was with Rick the night I bumped into you at Ruby's. He'd already told me that you were celibate. He admires and respects you for maintaining your faith."

"I can't believe Rick admires anything about a woman refraining from sex."

"Hey now, Rick's a good guy. He just loves women—a lot of 'em. I'm sorry you feel betrayed by me. I just knew you would eventually ask or someone would recognize me. A little piece of me wanted you to fail at your own juvenile game. You always boast about how you hate playing games, yet you played one with me, and lost."

"I didn't play a game, and I definitely didn't lose. I was concerned about the impression you would have of me if I started digging and questioning you about your profession."

"Speaking of impressions, don't you think I want to make a favorable one, too? How do you think it feels to be labeled and relegated, the way you did me, when you found out who I was?"

"You're right."

"Since our first date, I've done nothing but held you in the highest regard and treated you like a lady of your caliber deserves."

"You're absolutely right, Orray. I overreacted. Will you forgive me, please?"

"There's nothing to forgive. I'm just glad everything is out in the open and we're past it. Now can we go back in and get our party on? How 'bout a dance with this non-stereotypical basketball player?"

"I'd love to," Kennedy obliged, grinning from ear to ear.

Kennedy felt Orray's oozing sincerity, and she knew he was right. She'd started off on the wrong foot playing games, and realizing her childish ways made her feel horrible, but not for long. In a matter of seconds, all she could feel was a lustful heat, ignited by the strength of Orray's muscular embrace pulling her to the dance floor. She felt remarkably safe in his arms. His touch was stroft (strong and soft). She wanted to dance all night with him and never look back. Every time his grip tightened, she'd exhale in sheer pleasure. His six-foot-four frame engulfed her like a pig in a blanket. The good kind—one of those cute, little, salty Vienna sausages wrapped in flaky Pillsbury croissant dough. After a couple of songs, Kennedy returned to earth from her fieldtrip to heaven, joining the other girls at their table. Orray took a bathroom break.

Lexi and Ray had been mingling with their guests and were also just returning to the table. Ray immediately apologized to Kennedy for blowing Orray's cover.

"Kennedy, I'm so sorry. I wasn't trying to do that. I didn't know you didn't know... I..."

"It's okay, Ray. I'm cool; we talked about it. I overplayed the whole thing."

"Girl, you shole did," Reagan chimed in.

"Kennedy, I'm with Reagan. It could've all been avoided had you just asked the man," Lexi added.

"Not that it's anyone's business, but I'd planned on having that discussion with Orray tonight."

"All jokes aside though, Kennedy, that man is some kind of fine, and he paid! Baaaby, you hit the jackpot!" Amber congratulated, just as Orray walked back to the table.

"Oh, you're back," Kennedy said excitedly, kissing Orray on the cheek. "My turn now. I'll be right back, hon."

"Wait, Kennedy, I need to potty too," Amber said.

"What the hell am I going to do? I can't believe Orray is a professional basketball player!" Kennedy questioned Amber the second they hit the restroom floor.

"Girl, get over it. What's the big deal?"

"I'm not sure. It's all just starting to feel like déjà vu."

"You gotta let that go, boo. Continue to give him credit for what he's proven so far. Don't make problems that don't exist. He's a godly man, remember? He's saved. He values honesty and integrity.

"So what? Because he's doing what an upstanding man should be doing anyway, I should throw him a parade?"

"If that's what it takes to show your approval. That man hangs on your every word when you talk. So let his word be his bond, unless he shows otherwise."

"Amber, that's all good and well, but at the end of the day, he's still a panty-chasing NBA player."

"Kennedy, there are plenty of professional athletes who aren't interested in chasing thongs, and who understand what it means to be a faithful man. Granted, they're often the same ones who usually get trapped with a baby by a sideline hoochie."

"So the good athletes are the dummies?"

"You misunderstood my point. I'm saying groupies will chase a man from one corner of the earth to the other with the hope of having sex with him. And yes, there are those who are weak and consistently take advantage of hoochie sex. They fail to realize that all them road-rats are looking for is some good ol'-fashioned, professional ballplayer sperm. It's the ultimate thot paycheck. Cha-ching!"

"If you trying to make me feel better, Amber, you're sucking at it!"

"I'm just trying to school you on the game. Groupies are after one thing—the lifestyle an athlete or an entertainer can give them. Every now and again they might get some real play, and somebody famous might flaunt them around town for a hot minute. But in the end, they always get thrown out like old garbage, 'cause that's all they are, trash."

"And what makes you an expert?"

"Chil', please. You're not the only one with letters and a distinction behind your name. You might be a PhD, but I'm what's known as a GhD—a Gold-hoochie-digger."

"Amber, you're a certified nut!"

"But for real, give Orray a chance. He hasn't done anything to make you doubt him."

"The athlete thing has just got me twisted. All the talk players do in the locker room… I just don't want my name mentioned in that circle."

"Orray being a professional athlete is the least of your worries."

"It is, Amber. Now that his secret is out, I've got my own to worry about. What will he think when he finds out? Will he still be interested in me? Should I just tell him now? How in the world do I tell him?

"Kennedy, my advice is you tell him before he hears it in the streets, like you had to find out about him."

"What if he already knows? I would just be bringing up something we probably could've avoided discussing altogether."

"What if he doesn't?"

"It's not my responsibility to tell him."

"It is if you care about him," Amber coached empathetically.

"I do. He's starting to grow on me."

"Then give him the respect not to find out from anyone else but you, Kennedy."

"I don't know if I'm ready to suffer the consequences, Amber."

CHAPTER 11

Skeletons – Them Bones, Them Bones

"Kayla, I'm scared."

"Reign, you made your bed, now you have to sleep in it."

"That's cruel."

"It's not cruel. It's the truth."

"I know, but why you gotta be so mean about it?"

"I'm not trying to, Reign. I'm just telling you how it is. No need crying over spilled milk. My grandmomma always tells me to be careful about the decisions I make, because they'll always catch up with me."

Kayla's mother and father were missionaries who'd dedicated most of their lives to saving souls for Christ and helping others around the world. They believed a child needed good education and stability, so Kayla was left in her grandmother's care during their frequent absences. Consequently, most of Kayla's rearing was done by her grandmother, who also imparted many of her own traditional values and raw character in Kayla.

"Good for you and your grandmama!"

"I'm for real, Reign; the mistake has already been made. What are you going to do?"

"I don't know."

"I know this is tough; you need to pray about it."

"That's all you ever talk about, praying about something!"

"Well, if you don't talk to God about it, how do you expect to get the right answer? Pray without ceasing is the only way."

"I'm capable of making my own decisions, without praying about 'em."

"Reign, you gone learn the hard way."

"I should've prayed before I slept with Todd."

"Yeah, that would've been wise, too."

"Kayla, I need you as my friend right now. Not my mother or teacher."

"I'm here for you, Reign; I'll do whatever you need me to. The only person you have to answer to is God. Well, maybe not just him. I forgot about your mom, Ms. Amber, and Ms. Kennedy."

"Thanks, Kayla. I get the point."

"I'm not beating you up, I'm seriously saying that your decisions are only between you and God."

"I know."

"So have you thought about what you're going to do?"

"I got so many thoughts racing through my head, I can't concentrate. I feel like a fool not using a condom with Todd."

"It was a mistake. Now you know."

"I just never thought this could ever happen to me after only one time."

"That's what most people think. Have you told your mom?"

"Are you crazy, Kayla?"

"Well, who better to talk to than her?"

"You!"

"I can't tell you what to do. Really, she can't, either, but moms always tell you the right thing to do."

"I don't need her advice right now—that's all she ever gives."

"Reign, why are you mad at her? She's been there. Your mom knows how hard it is to raise a child alone. She knows what it's like to have a child with no husband, with all your friends and family looking down on you. I never told you, Reign, but my mother went through the same thing as yours. She wasn't married when she had me. The man that I call Daddy is not my real daddy. He's just God's gift to me and my mother. When my mom met him, she was twenty-two, and I was six. He walked into our lives and gave us everything we could ask for. But my mama still shared the stories with me of how people treated her when they found out she was pregnant at sixteen. My dad and her mother never judged her, though; they helped her create the life she wanted for herself, and me. That's why I'm so thankful to my grandmother and am obedient to my parents. My mom found a way out, but not every story ends like a fairytale. I wonder all the time who my real my dad is."

"You don't have any idea, Kayla?"

"No. My mom said it was just one of those things that happened. He was a boy she went to school with. She lost her virginity to him, and guess what?"

"What?"

"She got pregnant with me, her first time."

"I never knew that, Kay."

"Yep, that's why I don't want nothing like that to happen to you."

"Kayla, you know I know what it's like being raised by a single parent and not having a father around."

"Yeah, but at least you know who your father is."

"I know who he is, but what good is it if he's not in my life? At least you have a dad that's there."

"But he's not my real dad, Reign."

"What's a real dad, Kayla? A sperm donor? That's not a real dad. A dad is someone like the man you call Daddy. Someone who spends quality time with you during the week, comes to your recitals, hugs you when you're feeling down. A dad is the man you can depend on when you feel lost. He takes you to your favorite store and buys that pair of jeans that your mom won't buy because they're too expensive. A dad holds your hand on the first day of school. That's a dad. Not a man who got a woman pregnant because he was horny for a good time. You've got a dad, Kayla."

Kayla and Reign hugged and cried together. Tears streamed rapidly down Kayla's face as Reign's words pierced her heart and helped her to see the value of the man who'd raised her. She had in her dad all that Reign wished for. Reign's dad came by about as often as Christmas, and when he did make his annual appearance, it was never long enough to make a difference. He was always equipped with an excuse for why he couldn't stay longer than a split-second. "I just stopped by to give you some money. I'm on my way to work." His one-hundred-dollar drop-ins could never compete with what spending just an hour a week would have meant to Reign.

"Kayla, I wish my dad was half the man yours is. I guess you'll never know what you have until you lose it."

"Reign, you're my best friend. I'll love and support you to the end, no matter what. I'm worried about you."

"Don't, please. I can handle this."

"But you just told me you were scared."

"Because I don't know what I want to do."

"You thinking about not having it?"

"It's crossed my mind."

"Really, Reign, you ready for that?"

"What kind of question is that?"

"I mean, it just seems like it's gonna mess with your head ...to kill your child?"

"It's not a child, Kayla."

"You know what I mean."

"Who said I was emotionally attached anyway?"

"Why wouldn't you be? It's a part of you."

"I don't look at it like that."

"What if something happens?"

"Like what?"

"Like if something goes wrong and you can't have any more kids."

"This ain't 1917, Kayla. I'm not going in an alley to get rid of it. I'll be at a clinic with a real doctor."

"Yeah, but they could still make a mistake."

"Kayla, they know what they're doing."

"Well, what about abortion being considered murder?"

"I'm not murdering anybody, Kayla!"

"Yes, you are, Reign, and the Bible says, 'thou shall not kill.' "

"What am I killing? I'm just having cells sucked out. I looked it up on the Internet."

"Cells from a baby, Reign. They didn't tell you that on the Internet?"

"Whatever I decide to do Kayla, it's on me, not you. Like you said, it'll be between me and God."

"Have you even thought about keeping it or maybe giving it up for adoption?"

"Yeah, but I don't want to walk around pregnant for nine months and then just give it away to a stranger. That seems so dumb to go through all the pain and people talking about you, then put the baby up for adoption."

"That's not dumb. Some people believe that having an abortion is a sin, and would rather put the baby up for adoption than commit a sin by killing it."

"Will you stop talking about killing and murdering...?"

"Okay, abort the baby. Is that better?"

"What do you think I should do?" Reign asked Kayla after a moment of complete silence.

"That's not my place to answer, Reign."

"I'm asking you, so tell me."

"I don't know. It would be nice to have a godchild."

"It might be nice to be a mother, too, wouldn't it? I could hold him when he cries. Hug him and kiss his boo-boos when he falls. Rub his back when he's sleepy and cranky. Kiss 'em good night."

"Yeah, and you could change his diaper when he poops. Sit in the emergency room all night when he's sick. Pull every strand of your hair out trying to figure out why he won't stop crying. You could sacrifice a new pair of designer jeans to buy his medicine. You could cook, clean, and mommy the rest of your teenage years away."

"Uuuugh, I just don't know what to do, Kayla! Look what our parents went through to raise us; we turned out all right."

"No. You're wrong; our parents gave up their lives to raise us."

"Yeah, but the question is, do they regret any of it."

"My mother always says she regrets having sex at a young age, but she doesn't regret me."

"Kayla, this is the hardest decision I'll ever make. It's harder than my decision to lose my virginity."

"Have you told Todd?"

"Yeah, he said, 'I know you're not going to keep it.' "

"What?"

"Yes, he did. He made me so mad. We argued for hours."

"And then what?"

"And then he said it wasn't his."

"And?"

"And he wants a paternity test if I have it."

"Nasty dawg!"

"He pissed me off so bad, I told him he didn't have to do anything for me or this baby. When I said that, he totally changed. He apologized for everything he'd said and told me he was scared to be a teenage father. I read him up and down, like a book. I asked him if he thought I was on cloud nine over the thought of having a baby on my hip day and night; having to feed, bathe, clothe, and care for it. He promised he won't put me through nothing like that and said he'd stay by my side if I decided to go through with having it. 'I won't put all that on you, baby. I'm gonna be there for you and our baby. I'll help you get through this. It's just as much my responsibility as it is yours. We can be a family.' A family? He scared the crap outta me with that family stuff!"

"Maybe he's a good guy after all, Reign," Kayla smirked.

"He keeps telling me he feels equally responsible. I don't know what to believe because he's the same guy who told me he wanted a paternity test if I had the baby."

"I guess I need to give Todd more credit. I thought he was a dog."

"I asked him how he planned to take care of a baby without a job. He said he'd get as many jobs as he needed to, to do right by me and the baby. He kept going on and on about us being a family. That's what makes it so hard, Kayla. Todd is being supportive and wants me to have it. But, am I too young to be somebody's mama?"

CHAPTER 12

Guess Who's Coming to Dinner?

Who would've ever thunk Kennedy would be toiling over a hot stove, cooking for a guy she'd only been dating six months? He was truly deserving of all her kind gestures. He was sweet, considerate, and consistent. He even still held to his rituals of calling her every morning and evening. They were the kind of small deeds that made her want to love like she'd never been hurt before. But she had, and the threat of being hurt by love again was a road she wasn't ready to travel.

Orray had made it easy to trust again because he instilled such an overwhelming sense of security. He never gave her reason to doubt him. There weren't many men from her past she could say that about. In fact, there was only one man she could remember feeling secure and free as a bird with—Randall. He was all man: he knew how to talk, walk, and express love in a way that made her feel like the only woman on the planet.

His game was so tight he walked into Kennedy's heart like it was a sliding door. She fell hard for him. In her mind, if Randall took the day off, the moon wouldn't get hung at night. She loved him with an agape passion because all he ever gave her in return was unconditional love.

Regrettably, their love wasn't enough to make the relationship stick. Time quickly revealed they were on different paths and didn't desire the same fundamentals in life. He wanted to relocate to a different state. She wanted to take the positon at Crimson. They would've never worked, but Kennedy's heart didn't get the memo, and it took her forever to get over him.

The realization of losing Randall was like having a dagger slowly driven through her heart. It was a mental and physical pain that took residence inside of her. Some days the mere thought of him or hearing a song they both loved would give her heart spasms. At night she would lie in bed, clutch her pillow, and cry herself into a restless sleep.

It was a hurt she wouldn't wish on her worst enemy, and she never wanted to feel it again. But for the first time since Randall, Kennedy's heart was releasing the vice grip, and it felt good to find the will to let another person in. Having Orray over for a home-cooked meal was a huge step for Kennedy. He was the first man she'd invited into her home since taking her vow of celibacy. She took her promises to God seriously, and having dates over just seemed like an inevitable game of Russian roulette.

She was still human—a tempted structure of flesh and bones. Removing the act of sex from her life didn't automatically eliminate her sexual desires. She loved sex, and would feel her flesh crawling in lust when she had chemistry with a man. For Kennedy, being alone with a man was no different than an alcoholic touring a winery—something was bound to jump off.

Kennedy knew the lure of sex, and if handled irresponsibly, it had the power to become an addiction. It was a trap for the unmarried woman. The day she removed it from her life, she started to gain understanding of God's purpose for her future.

She stopped putting herself in positons where in-home dates would turn into random sleepovers. The absence of sex kept her feelings in check, and she was able to function more rationally. It was an awakening in her life where she honed in on her innate ability to read when a man only wanted sex. The red flag was him conveniently disappearing after the first date. Eliminating sex from her relationships gave her a new perspective on all the false signs of hope she gave herself with random men. She'd convinced herself that a man must care about her if he interacted with her in that way. Her intimate relationships had become so upside down, she'd confused lust with love for years. The twisted cycle morphed her into a sex addict, and there stopped being a relationship prerequisite for her to sleep with men; she did it because she wanted to. Some men had the power to turn her on just by looking at her, especially if he was a suitor she'd previously had a fling with.

The urge would sometimes be so strong she would neglect pressing responsibilities if just the likelihood of sex bordered on the horizon. She wondered if her insatiable desires were connected to anything that had happened in her childhood. Both of her parents played active roles in her life, and she had no looming memories of anything that would damage or cause her to be sexually wanton.

Initially, the thought of celibacy was a daunting, unachievable one. Watching AIDS statistics spike into a national epidemic was the turning point that made her take inventory of her reckless behavior. Frequent unprotected sex was never Kennedy's usual thing, but there were one too many occasions when she got caught up in the moment, and the condom was left on the editing room floor.

Becoming the executive director at Crimson also enriched her perspective. Avoiding sex as an adult was an amazing spiritual feat. In likeness, she couldn't imagine how difficult it must be for kids. She knew the combination of peer pressure and raging hormones would make it hard for any teen to make rational decisions about sex. Especially girls; they were most likely to be in search of some type of unfulfilled love, while boys were more hormonal junkies and just wanted sex because their bodies directed them to do it. Kennedy understood the dynamics and made it a point to help young girls embrace their bodies without the need to be sexual or find validation through a penis.

The sound of the loud ringtone startled her. "Hello," she answered.

"Hey, babe. What time is dinner?"

"How about seven?"

"Sounds good."

"Okay, that was easy. Well, I will see you then, Mr. Phillips."

Over the past six months, Kennedy and Orray had met out for their dates, or he'd pick her up, but they never stepped foot in her place. He always respected her wishes by walking her to the door, kissing her goodnight, and keeping it rolling. Things had gotten hot and heavy a couple of times, and only the hand of God helped Kennedy resist his touch. She was bound and staunchly committed to abstaining from sex until marriage. She was also mindful of what it meant to make a vow to God, and didn't want to feel his wrath or risk getting turned into a pillar of salt, like Lot's wife.

For the most part, it hadn't been much of a challenge to resist sex with Orray. When she was with him, her mind was constantly occupied by the agonizing decision of whether to tell him or not. Kennedy wanted to come clean, but was being held hostage by her fear.

"Oh, one second, honey. That's my other line. Hold on." Quickly swiping her iPhone, Kennedy answered, "Hello."

"Hey, Ken."

"Hey, Reagan. Gimme a sec. I'm on the other line with Orray." Clicking back over Kennedy said, "Okay, baby, I'll just see you when you get here. That's Reagan; let me see what she wants."

"Probably nothing, but go ahead. I'll see you at seven."

"All right. Kisses." She ended and resumed her call with Reagan.

"Okay, I'm back, Reagan. What's up?"

"Just checking in. What are you up to?"

"Nothing much, preparing dinner."

"Dinner?"

"That's what I said."

"You cooking?"

"I am."

"What's the occasion?"

"What makes you think there has to be an occasion?"

"Because you never cook, Kennedy."

"Well, I'm cooking tonight."

"For what?" Reagan asked sarcastically.

"You mean, for whom?"

"Giiirl, don't tell me you're cooking dinner for Orray?"

"Yep. Why do you sound so surprised?"

"Because."

"Because what?"

"Wait a minute, Kennedy. Don't say another word." Reagan clicked over to initiate a three-way call, adding Amber.

"Hello," Amber chimed in.

"Amber?" Kennedy questioned, confused.

"Yes, Kennedy," she responded.

"Reagan, you did not click over and add Amber to our conversation!"

"I sure did. And, Amber, girl, guess who's cooking dinner?" Reagan asked flippantly.

"Who?" Amber indulged.

"Kennedy!" Reagan shouted in amusement.

"Yeah, right," Amber said, cracking up.

"For real, Amber, I am cooking," Kennedy confirmed.

"Umm...Orray must be coming over?" Amber asked. Kennedy's friends knew her all too well. If she was standing in front of a stove it could only mean one thing—company was coming.

"What are you cooking, Kennedy?" Amber asked.

"I'm making chicken marsala with parsley potatoes, asparagus, and a salad."

"Are you serving wine, too?"

"Of course, Amber."

"Well, if you're planning to stay celibate, go easy on the wine, Ken."

"Thanks, Reagan. I will."

"It's a shame you can cook like that, Kennedy, but hardly ever do."

"I know, Amber. I haven't had anyone else in my life to enjoy it, and I don't like cooking just for myself."

"If I could cook like you, I'd have company every night."

"And your grocery bill would be high as hell too, Amber."

"Yeah, but if I had your skills, I'm sure someone would be happy to pay for it," Amber laughed.

"Kennedy, have you told Orray yet?" asked Reagan.

"No."

"Why?" Reagan shrilled.

"I haven't found the right time."

"Is there one, Kennedy?"

"No, there isn't, Reagan, but I just haven't had the nerve."

"Kennedy, if you don't tell him, somebody else eventually will. Then what?"

"I don't know. Look, Reagan, what am I supposed to do? Just blurt out something like that? Anyway, it's possible he could already know. I don't want to scratch a scab."

"And if he doesn't already know, Kennedy?" Amber poked.

"How many times do I have to say it? I'm trying to find a way to table the topic, but it just won't come out."

"Kennedy, you better tell him soon. Try to get around to it tonight," Reagan encouraged. "What time is he getting there? Are you dressed yet?"

"Seven o'clock and no! That's why I need to get off the phone, so I can get dressed."

"Okay, we'll let you go, girlie. Please think about how you're going to tell him tonight, though," Reagan reminded one last time.

"Bye, guys."

It was six fifteen by the time Kennedy ended her call with Amber and Reagan. She rushed to get dressed, but had a hard time deciding what to put on. She didn't want to wear anything skimpy, fearing it would skew the meaning of the evening. She even called Amber back to get her opinion on whether Victoria Secret's loungewear would be too suggestive. Amber was her usual unhelpful self, so Kennedy settled on a safe pair of fitted jeans and a cute top.

Orray arrived exactly at seven, wearing jeans and a button-down. He looked yummy, and seeing him confirmed for Kennedy that the evening would have to end early, or serious prayer would be in order to maintain a sex-free night.

"What'd you cook, bae?"

"For you? Chicken marsala, parsley potatoes, asparagus, and a mixed-greens salad."

"Sounds delicious. Any dessert on the menu?"

"You," Kennedy answered flirtatiously, noticing that Orray was gawking at her as if she were standing before him naked.

"Don't tempt me, Kennedy."

"I'm kidding, sweetheart. I made a red velvet cake. You wanna start with a glass of wine or a beer?"

"A beer sounds good. How long before dinner?"

"Just a few more minutes. You can turn on the TV or something—mi casa es su casa."

"So you know a little Spanish?"

"Very poco! Amber speaks it fluently, and in high school I picked up on a few words.

"You took Spanish in high school?"

"Two years, and two years of Swahili in college."

"Hujambo," Orray tested.

"Hujambo," Kennedy responded.

"Hibarigani."

"Enzuri. Wow, so you took Swahili too, Orray?"

"Yeah, it was one of those classes all the black people took."

"Same here." Kennedy smiled. "We were required to take a foreign language; I figured what's better than Swahili?"

"Maybe we can brush up on our skills together."

"Sure, I still have my Swahili-English dictionary," Kennedy reminisced.

"Me too."

"I used to speak it all the time when I was in school, but there was no one to practice with once I graduated."

"Same thing happened to me, and eventually it was one of those use it or lose it kind of things."

"Funny. Hey, babe, forgive me for not making the game last night," Kennedy apologized.

"No problem, I understand you had to be at Crimson for the recital."

"I'm glad you do. Otherwise, you know I would've been there."

"How was the recital?"

"Fantastic! Kayla came up with choreography that was spectacular. I was confused why she needed me to get so many props, and last night I understood why. She outdid herself; the production was like something a professional dancer would've put together. I'm so proud of her, and even happier that both of her parents were able to make it back in town to support her. She was more excited to see them than a kid on Christmas morning.

"And Reign sang a song she'd written about life decisions and how they affect us. Something powerful was moving in that child last night. The words went something like, 'I was born as a child of a child. The wise told me my life would be within reach of my imagination. The choices I make, the things I see, the goals I reach, will determine the span of every obstacle in my future.' I don't know—it was as if she was living through every word she sang. It was so touching; most of the audience was in tears by the time she finished."

"Isn't that what singers are supposed to do? Make the listener feel the emotion in the words they're singing?"

"True, but this was different, Orray. It seems like Reign is going through something life-changing. But I think it's good that at such a young age she has the presence of mind to realize how our choices in life can come back to haunt us."

"What does that mean?" Orray asked curiously.

"I'm just saying, sometimes we have to be honest about how our past has the power to affect our future."

"Kennedy, are you all right? You're getting really serious on me."

"Yeah, I'm just concerned about Reign and how her song seemed so personal."

"Kennedy, you're quite the woman. You give so much of yourself and you never seem to stop being concerned about the welfare of others. It's amazing to watch. I've never met anyone who cares about other people as much as you do. I see the mother, sister, and friend in you. You're the strength that every man wishes he could find in a woman. My love for you is growing every day." Orray stopped talking and began to gently kiss Kennedy.

Kennedy wiggled from his hold and whispered with her head hung, "Orray, I need to..."

"What is it, baby?" he asked sympathetically.

"I...I...I..."

"What?"

"I...think the chicken is burning!" Kennedy yelled as she ran off to the kitchen. The thought of coming clean to him was suffocating. *I can't do it! And now he loves me. Oh my God, not the "L" word! I haven't loved a man in such a long time. Did he really mean love or was he just caught up in the moment? Maybe I'm reading too much into this,* Kennedy thought.

"False alarm. The chicken is fine," Kennedy said, reentering the room.

"Did you hear what I said, Kennedy?"

"Yes, Orray, I'm glad that you admire me and—" Before Kennedy could complete her sentence, Orray's six-four frame was positioned in front of her, staring right through her eyes.

"I'm gonna ask you one more time. Did you hear what I said to you a moment ago? I said I love you, Kennedy," he repeated without breaking his stare, and holding her with a bear-hug grip.

"How can you be sure?"

"Kennedy, what are you so afraid of? I'm thirty-two years old. I think I know what love feels like, and I know I love you."

He kissed her again, passionately, and this time she kissed him back, after tenderly uttering, "I love you, too, Orray."

CHAPTER 13

Choices

Reign slowly approached the counter and softly said, "Hi, I have an eight o'clock appointment."

"Good morning," said the woman behind the counter. "How are you today?"

"I'm fine," Reign responded hesitantly.

"Okay, just take these papers, complete all the highlighted areas, and bring them back to me when you're done." From the stories she'd heard, Reign imagined the clinic would be drab and cold, with black paint on the walls. She was wrong. The walls were painted in a soft bluish-green hue and trimmed out in a buttery beige. The waiting area looked like someone's living room. As Reign began filling in her paperwork, she pondered how she'd ended up there.

The first section of the questionnaire asked for her name, age, and date of birth. Each section became progressively more complicated; one asking if she preferred general or local anesthesia. She had no idea of the difference, and skipped the question.

"Ma'am, I'm all finished," Reign declared, returning her paperwork to the front desk.

"Thank you. Just have a seat, and I'll call you back in a few minutes."

Reign walked back to the sitting area and sat next to Kayla. Kayla had been watching her the whole time, like a mother bird observing her own fly away from the nest. Reign had asked her to be there. She knew Kayla also wanted to be by her side and wouldn't judge her.

"Thanks for coming, Kayla," she said, her eyes filling with tears.

"I couldn't let you go through this by yourself," Kayla said, reaching for Reign's hand.

"I can't believe I'm going through with this, Kay."

"I know. This has to be the toughest decision you've ever made."

"It is."

Kayla and Reign lived on the west side of town, but decided to go to a clinic on the east side of town, hoping no one would recognize them. There were quite a few people sitting in the waiting room, and even though they knew none of them, it felt like everyone was looking at them. One girl seated near them appeared to be no older than eleven. A woman next to her was advising her on how to fill out the forms—must've been a mother or an aunt. Another woman near them looked no younger than twenty-five. She was sitting with a guy who kept rubbing her back and telling her it was going to be okay. It made Reign wonder if she would make the same decision had she been as mature as the woman. Why would someone her age have an abortion? What would make her not want her baby? It wasn't like she was thirteen or fourteen. She probably had a career, or at least a job, and the man with her seemed to be a willing supporter. Observing and attaching narratives to people in the waiting room forced Reign to evaluate if she was making the right decision.

"R. Curry, please come to the window," a woman summoned from behind the front desk. As Reign approached she asked, "Hi, are you R. Curry?"

"Yes," Reign responded in a terrified whisper.

"Okay, meet me at that door over to your left, and I'll take you back." On the other side of the door, she offered Reign a seat in a small, cold room.

"Let's begin with a few questions."

"Okay." Reign sat nervously, twitching in her seat and twisting her hair.

"How old are you?"

"Sixteen."

"Do you prefer the general or local anesthesia?"

"I don't know the difference; that's why I left it blank."

"There are a couple of differences, the first is price. In terms of the levels of sedation, you'll be completely asleep with general anesthesia; it also has more risks. Local anesthesia will just numb the area and you'll be awake."

"Will I feel anything?"

"Nothing under general, but you may feel some pressure and cramping with local."

"How much does it cost?"

"General is four hundred fifty dollars. Local is three fifty. Are you paying with cash, check, or money order?"

"Cash." Todd had only given her three hundred fifty dollars to cover the procedure. "I guess I'll have to go with local," Reign deduced.

"Okay, now, the next thing is you'll need to view a short video; after that, you'll speak briefly with a counselor. State law requires that we discuss all options with you before performing your procedure. Okay?"

"Okay." Reign wondered what the video would show. It lasted about five minutes and only covered alternatives (adoption or keeping the baby) to an abortion. Reign's eyes were glued to the monitor, but she didn't hear a single word of the video. She'd already made up her mind to go through with the procedure, be it right or wrong—she would take the matter up with God later. She just couldn't see how she would navigate through life as a teenaged mom. She sat in an unnerving silence for at least five minutes after the video ended. A counselor entering the room was like an oxygen mask on her face, breaking her racing thoughts; she could breathe again.

"Hi, Reign. I'm Mrs. Rampart. How are you?"

"Okay, I guess." Her voice softly quivered.

"Before we move forward, I'd like to make sure you understand the other options available to you."

"Yes."

"And you'd still like to have an abortion today?"

"Yes."

"Okay. Your paperwork indicates you'd like local anesthesia, correct?"

"Yes."

"Do you have a ride home?"

"Yes."

"Is your ride here with you now?"

"Yes." The counselor was used to young girls being afraid and only giving a sea of one-word replies. Reign was no different, and didn't impede her process.

"Okay, in a few minutes, the person who's driving you home can come back and see you before we get started. If all things go as anticipated, your procedure should be completed in about two hours. Your ride can stay, or can come back to pick you up."

The counselor left the room for a couple of minutes and returned with Kayla.

"How you holding up, Reign?"

"I'm scared, Kay."

"It'll all be over soon. Hang in there."

"Are you going to wait or come back when I'm finished?"

"I'm not going anywhere, Reign. I brought some books, and I might watch television out in the lobby. If I walk across the street to get a sandwich, I'll be right back. Don't worry."

"Kay, I don't know what I would do if you weren't here."

"Pray and ask God to get you through it."

"I love you, Kayla." Tears started to flow down Reign's face and Kayla grabbed a box of tissue nearby, handed her one, and draped her arm over Reign's shoulder. Kayla maintained her comforting hug until a nurse appeared.

"Hi, Reign. I'm Nurse Maureen, and I'll be with you every step of the way today, okay?"

"Okay."

"I need you to come with me to get changed and talk to the anesthesiologist."

In the exam room, Reign reluctantly changed into a faded hospital gown, knowing every washing of it symbolized a baby that had been aborted. Glancing down at her body, she was amazed at how quickly it had changed in such a short amount of time. Her breasts were engorged and sore. She removed her shoes and sat on an examination table, trying her best to remain calm and not cry.

A double knock at the door was followed by the quick entry of a man who politely introduced himself. "Hi, Reign. I'm Dr. Marks. I'm the anesthesiologist. I'd like to have a quick chat with you and have you sign some papers."

"Okay."

He began confirming the medical history Reign had documented on her questionnaire, asking lots of questions about her family and their medical history. After completing his questions, he handed Reign a form to sign, consenting to local anesthesia. Her hand shook so, she could barely sign a legible signature.

"You're going to be fine, Reign," Dr. Marks assured. "Just take some deep breaths and we'll take care of the rest." As Dr. Marks finished up, another doctor entered the room and introduced himself.

"Hi, Reign. I'm Dr. Cross, I'll be performing your procedure today."

"Hi."

Dr. Cross continued, "The procedure will be rather quick. You'll only feel a slight pressure and some cramping. Afterwards, I'll give you some at-home care instructions that I want you to be sure to follow. If you have heavy bleeding or other complications, please contact us immediately. The nurse will also give you a pack of birth control pills that I want you to start on this Sunday, so we can prevent this from happening again. Okay?"

"Okay," Reign said, looking down at her feet the entire time he spoke.

"In a few minutes, the transporter will come to take you to the room where the procedure will be done." Dr. Cross left the room, and as Reign sat waiting she began to shake, and her stomach felt queasy. It was frigidly cold, like someone had turned the air conditioning on full blast. She laid back on the table, rubbing her stomach, realizing that the brief sexual pleasure she'd experienced with Todd was not a fair trade for the predicament she was in. She prayed and asked the Lord to get her through it; and promised him it would be the last time. The sound of the door to the room opening made her look up.

"Hi, Reign, I'm Robert. I'll be transporting you for your procedure. All I need you to do is lie back, and I'll take it from here. Are you cold?"

"Yes."

"Okay, let me grab another blanket for you."

Robert pushed Reign down the hallway on what felt like the longest ride of her life. The corridor walls were so different from the ones in the waiting room; it was like she was in a different building. They were all stark-white painted cinderblocks—eerily institutional. Reign laid on the gurney, passing under row after row of overhead fluorescent lighting. She imaged she was riding the subway at night. She closed her eyes and began to lose reality of where she was.

Robert wheeled her through two metal swinging doors into the procedure room. Everything in the room was metal. There was a bright headlight-looking lamp attached to a metal stand, hanging over a narrow metal bed. To the right of the bed was a tray of metal surgical tools. It reminded Reign of something she'd seen in a Frankenstein movie and immediately made her apprehensive.

Dr. Marks appeared. "Okay, Reign, I'm going to begin your anesthesia."

"Okay."

"You're going to feel a pinch, then some pressure."

Reign's body jumped when she felt the injection in her thigh. She thought, *A little pressure? That hurt like hell!* After about three minutes, Dr. Cross came in. He was completely covered from head to toe in surgical scrubs and a mask. He looked more like he was playing the role of a doctor in a soap opera or something.

"Reign, I'm going to start the suction and you'll begin to feel some pressure. The more you relax, the easier it'll be." How'd he expect her to relax in a situation like that? There were at least three other sets of eyes standing by, watching everything. Her legs were propped up in stirrups, and all of her naked, lower body was exposed. She was embarrassed knowing a whole room of people were staring up her Vjay-jay. A noise started, and Reign realized it was the suction machine. Nothing could have prepared her for the horrible sound.

"I'm going to insert the tube now," Dr. Cross said as he pressed down on Reign's pelvic bone. Her body contracted even more, in fear. She tried to imagine other things, but nothing could take her mind off the tube being inside of her and the vacuum cleaner noise. The pressure grew more intense, and the cramping was like menstrual pains from hell. The more Dr. Cross moved the tube, the worse the pain became. She wanted to curl into a ball, and wished her mother was there to hold her hand.

"It's almost over, Reign," said Dr. Marks. Then suddenly, the suction noise stopped and dead silence fell over the room. "Okay, Reign. You can relax," Dr. Marks said, removing her legs from the stirrups.

Nurse Maureen walked to the foot of the table and placed a maxi pad between her legs. "This will catch any excess bleeding, sweetheart." She took another blanket and covered Reign's legs and feet. "It's all over now. Try to relax." She could see Reign's hands were still balled into fists.

"Relax, Reign. Give me your hand, honey. It's okay. Relax," Nurse Maureen kept saying over and over.

After a short time, Robert emerged and transported Reign to a cheerfully painted recovery room, where she dozed in and out of sleep for a couple of hours. She counted seven other girls lying in beds. *This is like being in an assembly line*, she thought. *One after the other, they take us in and suck our babies out.* Reign looked up to find Kayla standing next to her bed, smiling.

"Are you okay?" she asked.

"Yeah," Reign answered, feeling the tears building, but refusing to cry again. There were already seven other crying, groaning girls in the room; she didn't want to make eight. She snatched Kayla's hand and squeezed it. The whole scene was visually depressing—she needed to escape or she was going to implode. Kayla gathered her clothes and Reign dressed as quickly as her aching body would allow.

"Let's get out of here, Reign." Kayla grabbed her purse with one hand and clutched Reign's wrist with the other as they exited down a narrow hallway through a side door leading to the parking lot. It was over, finally.

CHAPTER 14

He Cheated

"Amber, have you seen the schedule for fall classes?" Kennedy asked, passing Amber in the hallway.

"I think I saw it at the front desk. Ask Kayla, she probably knows where it is."

"Thanks Amber."

"Hey, by the way, how's Orray?"

"He's fine."

"Just fine?"

"Yep, just fine."

"Any reason you're being so tight-lipped?"

"I answered your question, Amber. What else do you want to know?"

"A lot more than 'he's fine.' "

"Okay. Things are going good."

"Look, it's cool if you don't want to talk about Orray; just tell me. I'm not up for conducting a hallway interrogation today."

"Good, then don't ask me any more questions."

"One more thing…did you tell him?"

"See, you can't help yourself!" Kennedy chuckled and shook her head in annoyance. "No, I did not. I tried the other night, but I just couldn't."

"Why not?" Amber barked, while giving a look that made Kennedy want to cuss her out. Kennedy was sick and tired of people bringing up her stuff. It was her life, her relationship, and she would tell him when she was good and damn ready.

"Because! Things took a different direction. He told me he loved me."

"He told you what?"

"Uh-huh. L-o-v-e."

"Are you sure?"

"Hell, yeah, I'm sure. You must think I'm some kind of lunatic. I was there, sitting right beside the man, and he said he loved me."

"How did you respond?"

"I couldn't say anything; nothing would come out. Once he went into his speech about being in love with me, my tongue felt like a knotted pretzel."

"So you just ignored the man?"

"Eventually, I said, 'I love you' back. How could I not love a man like Orray? I'd be a fool not to. He's awesome in a way that doesn't exude he thinks he's God's gift to the earth. And best of all, he has a personal relationship with Christ. He's truly everything I want and need in a man."

"Chil', you sure you ain't gave that man none? You talking like a whipped woman."

"Amber, stop being foolish. I haven't given him anything. But not only have I gotten what I want in a man from Orray, I have what I need. Finding him is a testament to the fact that women should never settle for less than what we deserve. As women, we easily get mesmerized by the fantasy of the big wedding, building the house with the picket fence, and having the 2.5 children. We want it so badly, we start imagining that every man we meet or date could be our potential husband. When in actuality, I think women could be a lot happier and centered in the dating process if they focused more on what they need, rather than all the superfluous things."

"Easy for you to say, when you've found both."

"Well, I'm not taking the credit, because God knows it was nothing I did. God's time is not our time. When I was hyper-focused on what

I wanted, God didn't see fit to give it to me. Little did I know he was preparing me for the type of man that balances and complements me. Had I been impatient and settled for what I wanted, down the road I know I would've ended up with a huge emotional void in my life. Thank God for protecting babies and fools."

"Well, I wish he would hurry up and call my number, 'cause I feel like I've been waiting in line for my soulmate forever."

"Just don't give up, Amber; it'll come."

"Girl, I don't know if I'm more frustrated or desperate. Shoot, at this point, I'll even take a Mr. Right Now."

"You make me laugh! Trust me, I understand, Amber. I've felt like that too many times to count. Now, for the first time in my life, I've found someone I really trust, respect, and admire."

"Ken, you are really laying it on thick for this dude. It's getting harder and harder to believe you haven't let this brother grease you down."

"Honey, the only greasing we've been doing is on a 4-piece snack from Popeye's Chicken."

"Girl, stop! You gone make me pee on myself!"

"Seriously, though, withholding is not easy. Every time I see him, I want to wrap my legs around all six-foot-four of him. That man takes my body through some serious physical changes: my knees get weak, my vision blurs, my speech slurs. Ain't nothing easy about being celibate, but I just can't give myself to another man who's not my husband."

"But what if it sucks when you finally do it with him?"

"It's not all about sex, Amber; there's more to a relationship."

"Say what you want, Kennedy, sex and money are critical in relationships."

"To an extent, but they're only marginal components, because if they're all a relationship is based on, once they're gone, the relationship usually ends. There are so many other important things that actually ground a relationship."

"Like what?"

"Virtues like respect, honor, trust, love…"

"I'd rather have a man with money and the reassurance I'll be taken care of. I'll leave all those virtues for you."

"I feel like I'm beating a dead horse with you, Amber. All I can say is, money is temporary, and so is sex. Relationships require something far more substantial."

"Substantial is being able to attract new sex, with money provided by the old sex."

"Something is wrong with you, Amber; you need prayer."

Okay, well, pray for me, chil'."

"Don't you want to find that someone who completes you?"

"I can't believe you went there. Who needs a man for completion?"

"You're missing the point of the question. Completion is about being a team, and both people coming into the relationship whole. It's not about each being at 50 percent; it's about two people who are 100 percent, flaws and all, coming together for a greater good. Each must first be happy with their own cycle of life."

"Cycle of life?"

"The life that you create for yourself as a single person. The part of you that is completely independent of another being. Doing things and going places by yourself. Finding contentment in who you are and what you are, instead of seeking it in someone else. For you, Amber, it would be paying your own damned bills."

"If a man can't pay my bills, what am I gone do with him?"

"You don't need a man to pay your bills. You shouldn't be looking for handouts from anyone; that's ratched as hell."

"I'm not looking for a handout; just someone to help me."

"I don't understand why some women feel it's a man's responsibility to support them. Take care of yourself!"

"What good is a man, Kennedy, if he can't financially take care of his woman?"

"Sweetie, you're confusing girlfriend and lover with a wife. Commitment only comes with the latter; you're not entitled to anything as a man's lover or girlfriend."

"If I'm sleeping with him, I am."

"Baby, that's a pimp. You give him sex and he pays your bills in return. He's winning, not you. As a matter of fact, he could probably get off cheaper paying a prostitute for some booty, rather than paying your $700 car note every month. Allow a man to do what he wants for you, but don't expect anything."

"Kennedy, you live in that same fantasy world you just accused other women of being in."

"Yeah, and for the first time, my fantasies are coming true. Now, I got work to do." Kennedy ended the conversation abruptly and took off running past the front desk, heading for the bathroom. "Kayla, do you have the fall class schedule?" she yelled out.

"Yes, Ms. Kennedy, it's right here. Are you okay?" Kayla yelled back as Kennedy continued running down the hallway.

"Not really, I gotta use the restroom . . ." Quickly entering the bathroom and leaping into the first stall she saw, Kennedy realized she heard the sound of someone crying. "Who's in here?"

"It's me, Ms. Kennedy, Reign."

"What's wrong, sweetheart?"

"Ms. Kennedy, are you alone?"

"Yes. What's the matter? Come out and talk to me."

Reign walked out, her face swollen like she'd had a horrible allergic reaction to something. Her eyes were beet-red; snot and tears rolling down her face. She was noticeably disheveled, and her hair looked like it hadn't been combed in days.

"Tell me, Reign. What is it?"

"I'm okay."

"Clearly, you're not."

"For real, Ms. Kennedy, I'm fine," she said, with tears steadily pouring down her puffy cheeks like a rainstorm.

"If you were fine, you wouldn't be crying." Kennedy's words kicked Reign's crying into fifth gear. She was suddenly sobbing and hyperventilating. For a split-second, Kennedy thought she would have to give her mouth-to-mouth resuscitation.

"Reign, please try to calm down and tell me what's going on."

But she couldn't; Reign continued crying and moaning. Kennedy coached herself, *get yourself together, Kennedy. This is your purpose for being at Crimson. Help this child.* "Reign, I can't help you if you don't let me in. Breathe, Reign, breathe . . ."

"Ms. Kennedy . . . he cheated . . ."

"Who?"

"Todd."

"Todd. Who is Todd?"

"My so-called boyfriend."

"You have a boyfriend?"

"Yes . . ."

"How do you know he cheated?"

"Kayla saw him kissing a girl at the mall, and Kayla wouldn't lie."

"You're right; Kayla wouldn't. But maybe it was just a brotherly-sisterly kiss. You know, like a friendly peck on the cheek."

"No!" Reign snapped. "Kayla said Todd was rubbing on the girl's butt and kissing her in the mouth."

"Oh yeah, that ain't no sister. That boy cheating."

"I know that! What would you do if you saw Mr. Orray kissing another woman?"

"That wouldn't be appropriate for me to share with you, sweetheart. But it would be really, really bad."

"See?"

"But you do understand that Mr. Orray and I are on a different level than you and Todd?"

"How?"

"First of all, we're adults."

"That doesn't mean anything."

"Technically, you're right; we haven't made any verbal commitments or contractual obligations. So I guess you have a point. But you're still a child, and so is Todd."

"Are you having sex with him, Ms. Kennedy?"

"No, Reign, I told you. I'm waiting until I'm married. I want to be an example for you and the rest of the kids here."

"Ms. Kennedy, I'm not a child."

"In my eyes you are."

"This child's been having sex."

"Sex?" Kennedy asked, completely thrown off by Reign's abruptness.

"Un-huh…"

"Sex, Reign?" Kennedy inhaled deeply and did everything she could think to do to compose herself and keep from strangling Reign.

"Wow, you and Ms. Amber had the same reaction."

"Amber knows?"

"Yes, she made me tell my mother."

"How'd that go?"

"It was really hard, but I finally told her."

"What'd she do?"

"She almost killed me, but after she calmed down, she said a lot of the things Ms. Amber had already told me. She told me I needed to be on some type of birth control. Then she started blaming herself for not being at home more. I told her it wasn't her fault and that I knew she was doing the best she could."

"She sure is. Your mom is doing the best she knows how."

"I know, I don't blame her for anything. It's just sometimes you get caught up in situations when you have the freedom to do it."

"Reign, just remember that God gives us all the gift of choice, but it's important to pray and seek his guidance on our choices—before we make them, not after."

Reign was wise beyond her years and had spoken the truth about the perils of misutilizing freedoms. It was very easy for adults and children to become trapped in precarious predicaments, especially with sex.

CHAPTER 15

Betrayed

*K*ennedy's advice helped Reign to clearly see the error of her ways. Her decision to have sex before consulting God, and her lack of knowledge on protected sex, had led to an unwanted pregnancy. God had even sent his guidance through Kayla, but Reign's hard head wouldn't allow Kayla's spiritual wisdom to be heard.

"Are you on birth control, now?" Kennedy asked.

"Yes," Reign answered simply, unwilling to disclose further details. She couldn't bear revealing her pregnancy or withstanding Kennedy's biting words of disappointment. The abortion had been a tough choice for Reign, particularly with Todd's sudden excitement to embark on fatherhood. Ultimately, both agreed that neither were mature enough or equipped to become adolescent parents.

In the days following her abortion, Reign had become filled with shame and fear of what God's punishment would be for killing her baby. But after learning about Todd's TSA pat down on some girl in a mall, she grew more at peace with her decision. She was angry over her own naivety, and how she'd stupidly placed her hopes in an eighteen-year-old boy. On several occasions, Kayla had warned her Todd was just a smooth mouthpiece on the prowl for sex. Reign now kicked herself for not listening.

"Are you using condoms, Reign?"

"I don't need to; we broke up."

"Well, did you use them when you guys were together?"

"Sometimes."

"Why not every time?"

"When we first started doing it, I never made a big deal of it; Todd didn't either. So we just kinda went with the flow."

"Has he ever slept with anyone else?"

"He says he hasn't, but I don't believe him after what Kayla told me."

"What about the girl at the mall? Did you ask him if he cheated?"

"Did I? I sure did! I asked him to meet me at my house so we could talk face-to-face. When he got there, I told him I knew about what he did at the mall. He told me I wasn't his woman, we didn't have a commitment, and he could do whatever he wanted. He was like, 'I ain't put no ring on your finger.' I told him nobody said nothing about a ring, but he was the one who said he loved me." Kennedy was brewing with anger and outwardly appeared to be mentally drifting, but Reign continued. "I started crying and he said, yeah, I did love you and I still do, but I'm in my prime! I'm not trying to settle down and be with just one chick."

"If he were in front of me right now, I would break his—" Kennedy's sentence was interrupted by Reign's tirade.

"He went on and on about how he never promised me anything, but we could still be friends. Then the argument exploded, and things got a little physical. I yelled at him that he would've been a sorry, lowdown, dirty, good-for-nothing father anyway. He told me he just wanted a son, but had no intentions of being with me once the baby was born. He said I wasn't the first girl he'd talked out of her panties and wouldn't be the last. I felt like a rotten piece of meat—like some ol' dirty girl off the streets. He told me I was a dumb, ugly, nasty hoe. Something came over me, hearing him call me all those foul names. Before I knew it, I'd punched him dead in his stomach. He picked me up, grabbed me around my waist, and I hit the floor. Everything after that is a blur."

"Reign, did he hit you?" The rage in Kennedy's voice was palpable.

"No, Ms. Kennedy, he didn't hit me. He was just trying to keep me from hitting him again, but I fell when he grabbed me."

"Don't lie to me, Reign!"

"I'm not, Ms. Kennedy."

"You have to be careful handling a man like that. He's a lot stronger than you, and you could've been seriously hurt."

Reign didn't anticipate her breakup with Todd escalating into such a cruel and physical exchange. So much had happened during the argument at her house, she only vaguely remembered him leaving and asking, "Why'd you have to question me about another girl? Why did it matter? I always treated you like you were my only." He had a lot of nerve! He'd conned her out of her virginity, turned her whole world on its side, but couldn't figure out why she was bothered by his infidelity.

As she replayed the episode to Kennedy, Reign's tears wouldn't stop. It was the first time another person had inflicted that level of pain on her. In truth, Reign's agony was less about Todd's cheating and had more to do with him thinking so little of her, and expecting her to look past his indiscretions.

"I feel so broken, Ms. Kennedy."

"That's understandable, Reign. I would, too. We've all been there. We all know what it feels like to have our hearts splintered by that first love."

Reign just kept rerunning it all in her head: *What went wrong with us? What could I have done differently? Did Todd mean all those terrible things he said to me? Should I have been more understanding? Should I call him to apologize? Maybe I should've just kept my mouth closed about the girl at the mall. Will I ever see him again?*

Reign's cascade of tears started up again as she shared with Kennedy that Kayla had labeled Todd as a wild dog who couldn't be tamed. Kayla had maturely paralleled how obedience school didn't work for every dog, and assured Reign there was nothing she could've said or done differently to win over Todd.

"Kayla told me time would eventually heal my wounds, and I should be thankful God removed Todd from my life." Kayla often spoke like she'd lived a couple of lifetimes.

"Kayla's right, Reign," Kennedy affirmed.

"I know she is, but it's easy for her to say because she's not the one in the situation."

"Reign, tell me how long you and Todd were having sex." Kennedy's voice conveyed a harshness that dried Reign's tears right up.

"About eight months."

"Was he the only one you've ever slept with?"

"Yes."

"Are you sure?"

"Why are you acting like you don't believe me?"

"I'm concerned. I need the truth, Reign."

"Why?"

"If Todd was sleeping with other girls without using protection, and he did the same with you, you could have contracted something."

"Something like what?"

"Any type of sexually transmitted disease: herpes, crabs, HIV."

"HIV…isn't that AIDS?"

"It's what leads to AIDS."

"Todd didn't give me HIV!"

"How do you know?"

"Because we only had unprotected sex a few times."

"It doesn't take a few times. It just takes one."

"Todd is clean."

"HIV doesn't discriminate based on looks."

"Well, there's no way I can have HIV."

"That's not the way it works, honey. The disease doesn't skip over a person who looks clean, sweet, smart, young, or of a certain race. HIV has a mind of its own, and can be transmitted through sex. One of the only ways to stop transmission is by not having sex, or other precautionary measures, like using condoms."

"Ms. Kennedy, are you trying to scare me?"

"Reign, I'm not. I want to educate you. Statistically speaking, African-American girls between fourteen and twenty-four are the fastest growing population of new HIV cases. This is a serious matter."

"Todd said I was his first and only."

"And you said yourself Todd is a liar. Men say a lot of things when they're in the heat of the moment. That's why it's best to wait until you're in a committed relationship before making such serious, mature decisions."

"I know, but I trusted Todd."

"Looks like he mistook your trust for stupidity and weakness. It's a hard lesson to learn at your age, but trust is something you allow someone to earn. If you extend it without having proof that it's deserved, you run the risk of being manipulated. I think you gave Todd your trust a little too soon, Reign."

CHAPTER 16

On Bending Knee

*B*etween finding time for Orray, running Crimson, and being an attentive ear for Reign, Kennedy was usually beat by the time Saturday night hit. But since all the girls hadn't been out in a while, she was determined to join them for an evening of exhaling at Ruby's.

She especially wanted a chance to lay eyes on Alexis, who was going into her eighth month of pregnancy. Even in the fourth trimester Lexi was still sensual, radiant, and strutting her Naomi Campbell prance. She had a glow that only pregnancy and being in love could bring about. *Maybe one day I'll have that glow,* Kennedy imagined.

All of the girls were at a point in their lives where motherhood was a hot and heavy discussion, each fearing their biological clock would spontaneously explode any day, like a stick of dynamite. Reagan, surprisingly, was not an exception. She was consumed by her career, and most of the girls figured she'd never bear a child, but she, too, very much wanted one. Amber wasn't exactly smitten with the thought of having kids. But she was completely enamored with finding a baby daddy or husband who could pay a few thousand a month in child support and put her in a million-dollar house with a nanny in tow. The girl had major head issues.

Kennedy had strong opinions about how the degradation of society had tainted the institution of marriage. She believed lax value systems greatly contributed to generations of men having warped perspectives on what it really meant to be a father. And women (with their never-good-enough-attitudes) had a hand in discouraging men from being decent, present fathers.

Still, Kennedy had undoubtedly been bitten by the baby bug, and seeing Alexis made her hormones rage. She'd always dreamt of becoming a mom, but wanted to follow the Godly order of things. The opportunity to become a baby momma had presented itself ten times over. The guys she'd previously dated seemed more than willing to offer their sperm the minute they learned she was childless. The majority were oddly seeking fatherhood just as desperately as the women in her circle were pursuing motherhood.

Kennedy decided to take a long, hot, relaxing bath since Reagan wasn't due to arrive at her place for a couple of hours. A good soak in the tub with a couple of lit candles and a cold glass of Riesling was always the perfect antidote to clear Kennedy's head. The delicate sound of Jill Scott's crooning filled the bathroom, and the rush of the Jacuzzi bubbles hitting her body felt invigorating. They felt nearly as good as it would to have a pair of strong, black hands massaging every inch of her frame. The bubbles and Kennedy's sensual thoughts of a little something extra were the perfect storm to make her doze off.

Her ringing cell phone awoke her to a jarring return to reality. Knocking one of the candles into her sudsy, bubbling oasis she answered, "Hello?"

"Hey, gorgeous. What's up?" It was Orray.

"Nothing much."

"You sound like you were asleep."

"Yeah, my glass of wine, the warm water, and racy thoughts of you relaxed me into la-la land."

"Sounds soothing. Were those racy thoughts of me in a bedroom scene?"

"Orray!"

"I know, I know, sex conversations lead to sex. I can't help it, baby. I'm still a man. I've got to be one of the most patient men on the planet."

"You are—without contest, Orray; that's why I love you!"

"Anyway, you and the girls headed to Ruby's tonight?"

"You know it. What about you? You going out?"

"Yeah, I think me and Rick will kick it for a few hours."

He has to know, the relentless thought popped in Kennedy's head. *There's no way he could hang out with Rick this much and not know. Maybe Rick is keeping quiet because he doesn't want to seem like a hater. I can't take this. I've got to tell him.* "What are you boys getting into?"

"I don't know. We'll probably just have a few drinks and watch the game."

"Who's playing?"

"Lakers and Miami Heat."

Kennedy's basketball IQ wasn't what it used to be. Her hectic schedule didn't allow much time for sports, but since dating Orray she'd tried harder to be a part of his world, as he had so graciously blended into hers. At one time, she'd even been a hardcore Ohio State fan with a shameful crush on half the team. She was so busy studying each player's muscles and physique, she barely concentrated on the actual game. Orray changed that, and whenever he played, Kennedy only had eyes for him and his maneuvers.

On the court, it was only about her man. But was he really her man? Their commitment was more of an "understanding." Orray had not popped the proverbial "Will you be my girlfriend?" question, so only time would determine their level of commitment. *Why are men so afraid of commitment?* Kennedy wondered, only subconsciously listening to Orray chattering away.

Even without titles, Kennedy figured men had mastered the art of convincing women they were in exclusive unions. Preserving his own heart appeared to be a man's habitual goal. So, if he was kicking it with one woman and it didn't work, he could seamlessly hop over to the next without missing a beat. Reagan always said men were hopeless romantics at heart, and never limited themselves by the reins of commitment until they were convinced they'd found "the one."

"Well, have a good time, and tell Rick I said to keep you out of trouble."

"You mean the reverse. It's me who'll be keeping Rick out of trouble."

"Hold on, Orray; my other line is ringing. Hello?"

"Kennedy, you almost ready?"

"Hey, Reagan. Can you give me about half an hour?"

"What have you been doing?"

"I'm in the tub and on the phone with Orray. I promise; it won't take me long."

"Don't you talk to him enough? Get off the phone and get dressed!"

"Bye, Reagan. I'll see you when you get here," Kennedy diffused and quickly swiped back to Orray. "Babe?"

"Yeah."

He always sounded so sexy when he said *yeah*. In fact, there wasn't much he said that didn't sound good. He was just too good to be true. Day by day, a part of her held her breath, thinking there would come an hour when Orray would finally say, "This isn't working for me. I can't do the celibacy thing with you." Either that or he'd cheat.

She clung to the false sense of comfort given by her "no expectation" rule. It was a protocol that liberated her to stay in the present and allowed the inevitable to happen. Living in the moment made it easy to love Orray with an emotional freedom she'd not had in many seasons.

"Okay, hon. That was Reagan. She'll be here in thirty minutes, so I gotta run and get dressed."

"All right, baby, have a good time with the girls."

"You have fun too."

"Okay"

"Bye-bye."

* * *

The night was a little rare for Ruby's. The crowd seemed extra thick, like a convention or something was in town. There were a lot of players in the house from both the Cavaliers and the Dallas Mavericks. The music was real hyped, and it all definitely set the scene for a spectacular Girls' Night Out.

The girls had settled into their table, ordered drinks, ate, and cross-talked over each other like manic old biddies. Alexis was cuter than ever, sipping ginger ale and cranberry juice from a wine glass. Anthony had mixed the concoction, purposely making it resemble a sexy cocktail.

Amber was her usual hot self, igniting the attention of every man in the place, as half a dozen asked her for a dance or offered to buy her a drink.

"Hey, Amber."

"Hi, Reggie. How are you?"

"Good, and you?"

"I'm fine."

"I can see that," Reggie replied, giving his lips an LL Cool J lick that was a hideously failed attempt at looking erotic. His crusty lips resembled the crumbs at the bottom of a stale bag of Frosted Flakes. "Amber, you're one of Cleveland's best-kept secrets. Make sure you save me a dance."

"Okay, Reggie."

"He's such a lame," Reagan growled, watching him walk away.

"More like a cornball pest," Amber countered.

Right after Reggie, along came Alan, one of Ruby's nightly featured tools. "Heeeeey, Amber!"

"What's going on, Alan?"

"Nothing, just thought I'd come over and holla at you for a minute."

"Oh, okay."

"Can't get over how good you lookin' tonight."

"Thanks."

"Why you acting so cold, Amber?"

"Because I don't feel like being bothered with you tonight."

"Don't be so rude, Amber. You should be glad somebody's looking."

"I am glad; I just wish it wasn't you."

Amber had a tongue like a sword when it came to rejecting men. Instead of giving a nice brush-off like, "I'm just not interested, but thanks," she always went for the jugular. After her verbal assault, most men would need medical treatment, not limited to gauze and stitches.

The music slowed down with a little old-school Earth, Wind, and Fire, "Reason." It was a song that got Kennedy revved up every time she heard it. She scanned the crowd for a dance partner, and just as she was about to snatch Anthony, she heard a familiar voice.

"Kennedy. Is there a Kennedy Johnson in the house? Can I have everyone's attention, please? Kennedy Johnson?"

Kennedy froze in complete shock. It was Orray. He was supposed to be somewhere watching the game with Rick. What was he up to? Why was he at Ruby's? And why was he calling her to the stage?

As Kennedy approached, Orray shared, "Ms. Johnson, you thought I didn't notice you that first time I saw you at the gym, but I did. I noticed everything about you. You were wearing navy blue Nike sneakers, a navy sports bra, and matching blue and white fitted sweats. I even pretended not to see you when you fell off the treadmill. I watched your every move that day. I was awed by your beauty, even through the sweat. My brain kept sending me the signal that I needed to meet this stunning woman. There was something about you, girl."

Kennedy stood before Orray totally caught off guard, her armpits soaked from nervous perspiration. She thought she would faint, or worse, lose her mind. She hated being put on Front Street. Was he about to drop a bomb that he'd been traded and was leaving town? Before another possibility popped into her mind, Orray took a deep breath and continued.

"Kennedy, that first time I saw you at the gym, you'd packed up and left before I could introduce myself. You were quicker than Serena Williams on the tennis court." The crowd laughed.

"But God gave me another chance that night I saw you here at Ruby's. I asked my teammate, Rick, about you. He gave me the lowdown and told me who you were. So, I made it a point to introduce myself, and from your flirtatious hello, I knew I had you. Baby, you've truly made me a happy man. I love, respect, and cherish every part of who you are. I want you by my side as my helpmate. I want to grow with you, not just emotionally and financially, but spiritually, too. I want to be able to look at you thirty years from now and say, 'She's mine, all mine.' Kennedy, you're more than special to me—you're God-sent! I'm so thankful he sent me an angel. One I can love today, tomorrow, and throughout forever. I want to protect you when you're afraid and embrace you when you need to be held. I want to spend the rest of my life with you. Kennedy, will you marry me?"

Hearing the question she'd longed to hear for so many years, Kennedy leapt onto the stage into Orray's arms. Like a kid, she clamped her arms around his neck and her long legs around his waist. She kissed his lips over and over and over, finally uttering the words he waited to hear. "Yes! Of course, Orray! I'll marry you."

She felt her insides melting. She couldn't stop smiling. Her happiness was only thwarted by an involuntary shift in her thoughts, *When will I tell him? How will I tell him? I can't tell him now. He just asked for my hand in marriage. I could mess up everything!*

The music started blaring again. Orray grabbed Kennedy by the hand and led her to the dance floor. He pulled her into him by her waist, held her face in the palms of his hands, and kissed her as she had never been kissed before. They rocked back and forth, side to side, as the song played like a soundtrack to their love story. He dipped and twirled Kennedy until she could do nothing but giggle, laugh, and ultimately cry. It was the best surprise she'd ever had. That night, she was the happiest woman in the world.

CHAPTER 17

Let's Talk About Sex, Baby

"Good morning, Kennedy."

"Morning, Lexi."

"We took the initiative of ordering breakfast this morning," Amber chimed in.

"Thanks, Amber. I appreciate that."

"By the way, Kennedy, Reagan is on her way, too."

"Okay, ladies, what is this hen gathering all about?" Kennedy inquired, raising her eyebrows.

"Duh, last night, of course! Your future wedding plans! Remember, you got engaged?"

"Amber, can't I catch my breath first and just enjoy my engagement?" Kennedy asked laughing and partly giddy.

"No," Amber answered abruptly. "We need to start stirring up the coals and getting things hot."

"Lord have mercy! Can a sista catch a break?" Secretly, Kennedy was more than ready. She was out of her skin excited, and couldn't wait to toss around wedding ideas. But, if she acted too excited, she would seem more pressed and less cool to the girls. For so long she'd prayed and waited for God to send her a husband. Not a day passed when she didn't ask, *God, when will you send him?* Or look at a man and think, *Lord, could he be the one you made for me?* None turned out to be, until Orray. This time, she'd found "the one." The man who'd faithfully stood by her through a very personal and spiritual passage of celibacy. Finally, after thirty-two years, she was engaged and bursting at the seams in elation.

The girls were equally as excited, maybe more. Lexi and Amber taught Saturday morning classes, and as soon as Kennedy crossed the threshold of her office, there they were. They were perched on her desk, side by side, waiting to throw out questions like darts. Reagan was summoned to join in the round of twenty-one questions. Kennedy was mildly prepared for their first question, "When are you going to tell him?" Thank God they ordered breakfast; she was famished, and would need energy for the hell they were about to put her through. She tried to stall them by playing dumb. "Okay, ladies, what's up?"

"Well, Mrs. Soon-To-Be-Phillips. How are you this morning?" Lexi asked.

"I'm fine. Actually, better than fine, Alexis. You?"

"I'm doing great, just ready to drop this little load I'm carrying."

"Little? Lexi, I think that load in your belly would be too much for even a dump truck," Amber poked sarcastically while rubbing Lexi's plump belly.

"Shut up, Kennedy," Amber smiled proudly.

"And, Ms. Amber, what is it you'd like to know on this fine Saturday morning?" Kennedy provoked.

"Stop messing around, Kennedy; did you give him some last night?"

Kennedy rolled her eyes in disbelief. "No, Amber! You're joking, right?"

"Amber, get off Kennedy's back, and give her a moment to soak it all in. The engagement is just a step in the process. Nothing has changed. Kennedy's still planning to wait until they're married," Lexi declared.

"She can be a fool if she wants to, Lexi. I ain't buying no cake until I taste the frosting."

"Where did you get that dumb line from, Amber?"

"Ain't nuthin dumb about what I said, Kennedy. I like cake, I like men, and wouldn't take either home without sampling first. I'm just saying." Reagan entered the room just as Amber was wrapping up her analogy.

"Hey, Reagan," Kennedy beamed.

"Well, well, well...good morning, the soon-to-be Mrs. Phillips," Reagan greeted Kennedy, smiling from ear to ear.

"Nice to see you here so early."

"There's no way I was going to let you girls have this conversation without me, Kennedy."

"We could have conferenced you in by phone."

"Oh, no you couldn't have. You think I'd risk missing all this tea we're about to sip?"

"Reagan, girl, there ain't no tea to sip. Do you know she didn't break that man off a piece last night, even after his public, romantic proposal?"

"Amber, have you ever made a decision that wasn't centered on sex or money?" Kennedy asked.

"That's a good question, Ken; let me think on it."

"Well, I, for one, am not going there today with you, Amber," Reagan began. "First of all, you need to know relationships aren't all about money and sex. There's so much more to male-female intimacy than a roll in the hay or the size of a man's wallet. You need to get past that college girl stupor you're stuck in. Building a lifelong partnership with someone has everything to do with creating a bond that outlives hot sex and the physicality that fixates both people in the beginning of a relationship."

Interrupting Reagan, Kennedy raised her hand in the air in a halting motion. "Reagan, you're wasting your time. I've been through this with Amber more times than I shower in a calendar year, but she's hell-bent on making sex and money the priorities in her relationships."

"Come on, Reagan and Kennedy! Y'all know a man's gotta at least be able to handle his business in the bedroom."

"True, but there's a total package evaluation that counts for so much more: emotional attachment, the ability and desire to commit, sexual compatibility, religious values...the laundry list goes well beneath the surface," Kennedy argued.

"Okay, Dr. Ruth Kennedy."

"For real, Amber, if the chemistry is there, you can talk your way into good lovemaking."

"I don't have time for talk, Kennedy. I need him to come correct with some serious motion in my ocean."

"Thank the Lord. She finally admitted it. That old thang between her legs is so worn out, she's now even referring to it as an ocean," Reagan joined in.

"Whatever, big mouth Reagan. Just remember, the ocean is a beautiful and fun place to be. Ain't nobody turning down a trip to the ocean. It's a lot more exciting than slumping down an old, dark, cavernous cave—kinda like what you got! You and Ken kill me, actin' like y'all are so into the relationship thing now, when just a few years ago it was all about sex for both of you."

"I never claimed that at a point it wasn't just about sex, but even then I stuck to my convictions that there's more to a relationship," Kennedy reminded Amber.

"Yeah, and now you and Reagan are so wise and evolved, right?"

"No," Kennedy answered. "There just comes a time you realize in order to have something long-lasting, you've got to go beyond the superficial—and sex is undeniably superficial."

"So why try to pretend you were never sex-crazed, Kennedy?"

"Wait, did I say I wasn't, Amber? I don't remember those words leaving my mouth. I've had my struggles with sex. Hell, you can even label it an addiction. But everything I went through is the explanation for why I changed my lifestyle and evaluate relationship choices more carefully. It all made me realize I needed and deserved more. Not just some motion in my ocean. I can do that all by myself, anyway."

"Okay, ladies, let's not venture on the topic of self-gratification," Lexi bashfully whispered.

"Amber, what it boils down to is I reached a place where I was determined to say no to sex until I said yes to marriage."

"So now you trying to sell me on the notion that celibacy helped you nab a husband?" Amber heckled.

"That's not what I'm claiming. I just happened to find someone who didn't mind waiting and honored the path I'd chosen for myself. Abstinence allowed us to authentically get to know one another instead of confusing sexual heat with heartfelt love."

"That's so incredibly beautiful," Lexi gushed.

"Oh, don't you have a baby to go drop off somewhere, Mother Theresa?" Amber playfully snapped at Lexi.

"Don't hate on Lexi because she recognizes a true, mature courtship and all you know is true lust."

"You're getting lamer by the second, Kennedy."

"I got Orray by waiting, Amber, so I can't be that lame."

"Sorry, Kennedy, you didn't get Orray because you waited, you got him 'cause he crazy. Any man that marries you has got to be cuckoo for Cocoa Puffs."

"Amber, you're full of jokes today, huh?"

"Who said I was joking? I knew that brutha was crazy when he put that big ice cube on your celibate ring finger."

Lexi jumped in again, "Oh my God, we didn't even touch on the ring! Just look at the size of that freggin diamond on your hand, Kennedy."

"If I'd known waiting would've gotten me a four-carat diamond, I would have stayed a virgin," Reagan proclaimed.

"I'm just thankful Orray loved me enough to wait with me," Kennedy said.

"I wonder what made him wait. I know it was killing him," Amber queried.

"I think it had a lot to do with where he is in his life. He's trying to grow spiritually, too. Not to mention, he knew he had a good woman that he didn't want to lose."

"You got that right, Kennedy!" Reagan shouted, giving Kennedy some dap in agreement.

"Let's just keep it one hundred. I love the man, but in all honesty, Orray probably waited because he had done so much dirt in his past. He was kind of like a camel who'd stored up enough reserve for that long trek through the dry desert. Trust me, girls, Orray ain't nobody's saint.

I remember the time he had a game here in Cleveland, and we ran into a groupie he'd slept with when he played for Dallas. Something about the way he handled that encounter made me curious. So, I just asked him straight up if he had a woman in every city, and his verbatim response was, 'Just about.' I started to break it off with him that day, but my gut told me he was bigger than his past transgressions."

"Damn, your man was like that?"

"He really was, Amber. I just met him at the right time; it was God's timing, and certainly not mine. I simply caught him at a juncture in his life when he understood there was more to it than basketball and sex."

"See, that's the key, Kennedy; you didn't try to change him into what you wanted," Reagan acknowledged.

"You're right. I didn't want to change him. I didn't make him wait, and I sure as hell didn't force him into a commitment. He was ready for everything he submitted to, and that's why he was able to hold out. You can never make a man give more than he wants or is prepared to give."

"Guys do what they want, even if it means passing up a good woman. I'm glad Orray had his head on right, Kennedy," Alexis added.

"Look how scared Johnny got when you tried to push him before he was ready, Amber," Kennedy reminded. "That boy put on his Reeboks and did a hundred-yard dash right out of town."

"I'll admit to that one, and I agree you can't change a man. But you sure can emphasize how good of a sale Nordstrom's is having or that your car note needs to be paid," Amber countered flippantly.

"Okay, stop right there, Amber. Did you guys have any idea Orray was going to propose last night?"

"We did."

"How did you find out, Lexi?"

"Orray called and told me to make sure you were at Ruby's Friday night because he was going to ask the big question."

"Are you serious? So, you all knew?"

"Sure did, Kennedy. Your momma and daddy know, too. Orray did it the old-fashioned way and called your dad to ask his permission. Your mom is probably sitting on the edge of her seat waiting for your call," Lexi explained.

"I did. I spoke with her this morning. I can't believe my mom was able to keep it a secret and didn't drop one hint. Reagan, how were you able to keep those flapping lips zipped? You too, Lexi, I can't believe you didn't tell me!"

"I wasn't going to let that one slip."

"Is that why you were avoiding me all last week, so it wouldn't leak out? Wow, now it all makes sense! That's why Ruby's was packed wall to wall last night. When we arrived, I noticed there were a lot of NBA players in the house, but I didn't think anything of it."

"Don't you remember how Reagan kept pressing you to wear something other than jeans?"

"Alexis, I guess I didn't put two and two together, and I'm glad I didn't. It was the most unexpected surprise of my lifetime."

"Girl, that's a good man."

"He sure is, Alexis."

"I was so impressed by the way he did things."

"You were impressed? Honey, I was shocked out of my mind. Who helped him pick out the ring?"

"Reagan, of course," Lexi said. "Guess I'm too conservative for your taste, and Amber's too hoochie. He figured Reagan would be his best shot at matching your taste. Do you like the ring?"

"Are you kidding me, Lexi? This stunner on my left finger is as good as it gets. I love the ring, but I love the man even more."

"I haven't seen a ring that clear and brilliant before."

"That makes two of us, Lexi. I've never seen anything like it. Reagan, my friend, you did a remarkable job. How will I ever repay you?"

"Actually, Orray did most of the picking; I was just the yea and nay woman. Had he picked a gaudy, ugly, mountain of diamond dust, I would have pulled his coattail, but his taste was exceptional. When he found the ring he wanted, he looked at me and said, 'That is the one, Reagan. I know Kennedy will love it.' He was right!"

"When he opened that box on the dance floor ... girl, I thought I would pass out. I couldn't believe it was happening. For a minute, I couldn't even get 'yes' out. I was so mesmerized by the proposal and the ring. Something in me almost asked him, 'Are you sure you're ready to do this?' "

"Kennedy, that man loves you. Look how much trouble he went through to create the element of surprise. And he took a risk doing it in a room of mostly strangers. Now, that's love."

"Lexi, you are such a sucker for love and romance," Reagan accused. "Don't you know he already knew Kennedy would say yes?"

"He sure did know I'd say yes. And I can't wait until our honeymoon so I can say yes every night," Kennedy bragged.

"See, I knew you were still sex-crazed," Amber mocked.

"Get a life, Amber! I was celibate; I didn't dry up like a piece of old fruit."

"Yep, you just need a little rain on you," Amber added.

They all laughed so loud it could be heard echoing down the halls of Crimson. Then, Reagan silenced the laughter. "Kennedy, did you tell him?"

"No, and I'm not going to talk about that right now. This is a happy, celebratory occasion," said Kennedy.

"Truthfully, will you even tell him at this point?" Reagan asked reluctantly.

"Why should she?" Amber opposed. "Why now? She could screw up everything."

"Amber, that's the craziest thing I've heard all month."

"It's not crazy, Lexi. Some things are better kept quiet."

"I can't believe you're saying that, Amber."

"And Amber, back when they began dating, weren't you the first to encourage Kennedy to tell Orray?" Reagan furthered.

"That was before the marriage proposal and the millions of dollars at stake, Reagan," Amber snidely responded.

"Amber, you don't enter a marriage lying and keeping secrets!" Alexis snapped.

"Why the hell are you all talking about me like I'm not here?" Kennedy barked angrily. She couldn't figure out why everyone had such an insatiable need to treat her business as if it were theirs. "Alexis, you think I should tell him. Amber, you think I shouldn't, and Reagan, you believe in straightforward honesty. I've got news for the three of you—I will handle this the way I see fit, when I see fit. And who the hell made it a crime not to share every detail from your past? What I did before Orray doesn't concern him, or anyone else, for that matter."

"He has a right to know, and you need to tell him, Kennedy," Alexis sweetly stressed.

"No, she doesn't, Lexi. She doesn't have to share everything with him," said Amber.

"Amber, I agree, but this is one that she does have to put out there," Reagan said.

"No, I don't, Reagan."

"What if he hears about it on the streets, then what?"

"That's a chance I'm willing to take, Reagan."

CHAPTER 18

Test of Time

$\mathcal{A}$ few weeks after getting engaged, Kennedy hit a brick wall of exhaustion. Every joint ached, every nerve throbbed, and every muscle felt strained. Planning a wedding was a sport she wasn't physically conditioned for. Selecting flowers, a reception site, wedding favors, the band, deejay, food, alcohol, and a myriad of other details were getting the best of her.

Do I want ocean blue, pastel blue, greenish-blue, or turquoise? She was not prepared for all the planning and decisions she alone would have to make. Thank God for Moses, her wedding coordinator. He was demanding and a little irritating, but the best a whopping 20 percent fee could buy. When a friend recommended him as the crème de la crème of wedding planners, Kennedy expected a stereotypical movie persona that would be darting around, popping his lips, and snapping his fingers. 'Ms. Thing, oh no, that dress choice is dreadful! That will never work! You need to get your fashion life together, baby!' But Moses was the antithesis of that eccentric character in her head. He was professional, resourceful, and a class act.

Albeit, all the planning had started to become more of a pain than pleasure, and Kennedy's body was sending her a signal it needed downtime.

So, she loaded a few of her favorite songs on her iPod and drove over to Crimson's dance room to stretch and find some solitude. Taking deep breaths into her lungs and releasing each slowly through her mouth, she could feel her heart rate lowering and the stress peeling away.

"Hey, Ms. Kennedy," Reign said, entering the studio.

"Reign! What's up, little lady?"

"Hi, Ms. Kennedy," Kayla said, following behind Reign.

"Wow, to what do I owe the pleasure of seeing both of my favorite girls today?"

"Reign and I need to work on some routines for the junior dance class," Kayla answered.

"Show me what you have so far; maybe I can help." Reign began to dance the first sixteen-counts of the routine. She was popping so hard, it looked like her butt cheeks would fall right out of her shorts. "Reign, Reign! Baby, slow down on the gyrations, honey."

"Ms. Kennedy, stop being so old-school. You got a better suggestion for the first sixteen counts?"

"Let me see... how about this?" Kennedy demonstrated her best moves, trying hard to show Reign and Kayla she still had it.

Kennedy's choreography got Reign excited, "That's nice, Ms. Kennedy! Real nice. Okay, let's add these sixteen to it." Reign worked her body in a way that made it clear she was a naturally gifted dancer. She had skills that no dance instructor or dance class could impart. Her talents were God-given.

"Heeey, I like that, Reign!" Kayla said, snapping her fingers while looking in the mirror, trying to mock Reign's movements. "Let's add a pirouette to the end of that, too," Reign said, spinning around like a human tornado.

Reign put on the music and challenged Kennedy, "All right, Ms. Kennedy, let me see you try this one."

The three danced, mixing jazz, contemporary, ballet, and hip-hop. Before they knew it, hours had passed, and they were dripping buckets of sweat. When it was all over, Kennedy felt like she needed an ice bath, hot compress, heating pad, four Motrin, and a full body massage. Reign and Kayla had pushed her well beyond her geriatric limits. They had more energy than a 12-person dance troupe.

"Okay, girls, stick a fork in me; I'm done. I am beat!" Kennedy relented.

"Me too." Reign exhaled, falling face down on the floor. "Ms. Kennedy, this was so much fun. Thanks for helping us."

"The whole magic behind dancing lies in creativity and collaboration," Kennedy replied.

"I never even looked at it like that, Ms. Kennedy. I always thought dancing had more to do with skill than creativity," said Kayla.

"Performance and skill are a part of creativity. Both allow you to express and experience different artistic forms. It doesn't matter if you're dancing, singing, acting, or writing—creativity is what makes your creation different from mine, even if we're working on the same piece."

"Thanks, Ms. Kennedy."

"You're always welcome, Kayla."

"Yeah, we appreciate you, Ms. Kennedy," Reign echoed. "By the way, I never thanked you for letting me get snot all over your shoulder the other day."

"No problem, Reign. Over the years, I've messed up quite a few of my girlfriends' blouses, too."

"Reign, that's so disgusting," Kayla, said with a nauseated look on her face.

"Reign, I've been meaning to revisit that discussion with you, anyway," Kennedy appealed.

"What about it?" Reign responded innocently.

"I'm gonna run take a shower while y'all talk," said Kayla. "This way I don't have to worry about Reign hogging up the only mirror."

"Okay, Kayla. So, Reign, how are things going since we last talked?"

"Okay. I guess."

"Have you talked to Todd?"

"No, I decided it was time to let that one go. He never meant me any good. He figured out I needed extra attention with my mom being gone so much and all. He just used me."

"Have you thought about all the things we talked about?"

"Like what?"

"I want you to get tested for sexually transmitted diseases, and it's time you start getting regular pap tests."

"Ms. Kennedy, I'm too young for all that."

"Reign, once you start having sex, you take on the responsibility of being a woman, and being a sexually active woman means HIV testing and regular paps. If you're going to be sexually active, you've got to be sexually responsible, too."

"I'm not sure if I need it."

"Well, I'm sure you do, especially knowing you and Todd had unprotected sex. Didn't you tell me he was sleeping with other girls? You know, that raises the odds that he could have contracted something from another person and passed it to you."

"I'm not having sex again until I'm married."

"That's a good thing, Reign. I'm glad to hear that such a hard lesson brought you to a positive resolve."

"I'm for real. Sex is not for me."

"Reign, sex is an incredible act when it's ordered the way God intended, and with the person he intended. God meant sex for pleasure and reproduction. At the same time, when it's done prematurely or for the wrong reasons, it can certainly become one of those things he ordained for good that turns out badly. I would never try to convince you that sex is not gratifying, and I know once you say yes to it, it's hard to reverse. That's why it's important to have other interests and keep your mind occupied with constructive things. There's some truth to the old proverb, 'an idle mind is the devil's workshop.' It's hard to think rationally when a man's telling you how good something feels or how good you feel. The lustful impulse is what sets the stage for unprotected sex and unplanned pregnancies."

"Ms. Kennedy, I think the HIV thing is scary; just hearing you talk about it makes me want to use condoms."

"You should! It's a serious, deadly disease. It's one of the things that scared me into celibacy."

"So, why don't more people, including myself, avoid unprotected sex?"

"Well, honey, once hands get to rubbing, tongues start licking, and clothes go flying off, people get caught up in the moment…and putting on a condom is the furthest thing from the brain."

"I know, look at me."

"Exactly. And most women who find themselves infected or pregnant are just like you. They don't demand condom usage, and allow men to get away with thinking not using one is acceptable. I'm not solely blaming men, because I believe more would use condoms if women simply required it. We have enormous power over the situation, but we forfeit our control and yield to our own weaknesses. And we very frequently give it up the first night without weighing consequences. Women talk a good game publicly, among their friends, but if most were asked in a secret confessional, they'd probably admit to not seeing an issue with first-date sex."

"Why does it matter if it's the first date, second week, or first month?"

"Reign, I don't care how beautiful or fine a woman may be, once she has sex with a man she's no different from any other woman. Holding that one thing about you sacred—for as long as you can—will always make you special. When you give it up the first night, you miss the privilege of feeling unique and making a man earn that treasured part of you."

"Wow. Ms. Kennedy, you be making me think. I'm so happy you care about me."

"I do, Reign, and that's why I cannot stress enough how seriously sex should be taken. It requires a maturity and understanding you couldn't possibly have at sixteen."

"You got a good point. Maybe I should get tested for HIV, but I'm scared, Ms. Kennedy!"

"I was too. I remember my first test; my heart was racing, and I had a headache the whole two weeks I waited for my results. I prayed every night for God's favor and mercy. I may have even said some desperate prayer like, 'Lord, if you let this test be negative, I promise I'll never do it again.' When I received my negative results, I was so grateful to God, I honored it with a vow of celibacy that same day. I swore to him and myself I would never go through the agony of anticipating another positive outcome. And not that marriage is a sure way to avoid HIV, but it's a lot safer and smarter than sleeping with every guy you date. The process can be terrifying. How about you, me, and Ms. Amber get tested together?"

"That sounds good, Ms. Kennedy. But why do you need another test?"

"Just to make sure. Anyway, Orray and I promised each other we'd get tested before the wedding."

"What if Orray's comes back positive? Will you still marry him?"

"I don't know, Reign. I'll have to cross that bridge if I reach it. My prayerful hope is that I won't."

"That would be a tough decision, Ms. Kennedy."

"It sure would. But if he's infected, he hasn't put me in danger, because I haven't slept with him. Though, I have a great likelihood of contracting the disease if he's positive and we have intercourse. How about we take one step at a time and start with scheduling a test."

"All right, Ms. Kennedy. I'll feel much better having you and Ms. Amber there with me."

"You should schedule a doctor's appointment, too, with a gynecologist. If you don't know one, ask your mother, or I can refer you to one."

"You mean a girly appointment?"

"Yes," Kennedy answered with a deep chuckle.

"Okay, I'll do that too, Ms. Kennedy."

"Why don't we get showered and changed and go for our test this afternoon? I can ask Amber if she's open, if you're up to it."

"Will she want to?"

"She won't have a problem going, Reign. She gets tested every six months."

"It doesn't scare her?"

"I don't know, ask her." Kennedy couldn't answer the question for Reign. She didn't want to give her the impression that it was cool to have unprotected sex as long as she was regularly tested. Amber was grown and would have to filter that question for herself. "See you in a minute, Reign; just meet me in my office once you're dressed."

Amber and Kennedy decided to take Reign to the free clinic, where no one would know her and she could test anonymously. There was a man in the waiting room scratching his crotch like he'd been stung by a 100 yellow jackets—must've been crabs.

"What's wrong with him?" Reign asked, frightened.

"He probably has crabs, the clap, or something," Amber guessed.

"Ms. Amber, do you use a condom every time you have sex?"

Amber nearly choked on her spit. Kennedy knew it was coming, but Amber was caught off guard by Reign's sucker punch to the gut question. Amber was like a big sister to Reign and they'd broached the topic of sex many times, so Reign already knew Amber was sexually active. Amber paused and took a bottomless sigh before answering.

"Umm, I would say I use a condom 99.999 percent of the time, but I won't lie, I've slipped a few times." Kennedy knew fireworks were going off inside of Amber's chest, but on the outside she was cool as a polar bear's toenails.

"That's not good, Ms. Amber," Reign retorted.

Kennedy admired Amber's integrity with Reign. She doubted if she would've been able to respond as candidly, had she been in the same hot seat. Amber's honesty was refreshing, because kids had a knack for sensing a lie, even when they pretend not to.

"You're right, Reign, not using a condom should never be an option when you're sexually active."

Huh, it's getting so bad married couples are using condoms. It's dreadful to think about mates cheating on their spouses, down-low brothers, sistas out in the streets looking for validation they can't get at home, sistas settling the infidelity score with strangers. Sex has become a game—and a fatal one. In her head, Kennedy silently tossed around those thoughts and so many more—not wanting to expose Reign to the harsher realities of life.

"A woman should buy her own condoms. If a man says he doesn't have one, then she can go to her trusted stockpile. Now, if he just refuses to use one, that's when it's time to start walking toward the front door," Amber schooled Reign.

A stately looking nurse dressed in purple scrubs stood in the entryway leading to the testing rooms. She yelled, "Dixon! Ebony Dixon!" Amber rose from her seat and walked toward her.

Kennedy looked at Amber curiously, and before Kennedy could ask, Amber snapped quietly, "Shut up. Anonymous!"

Then the same nurse called out, "Lisa Brown!" Kennedy realized she was Lisa, after spotting Amber's aggressive motion for her to approach the nurse. Kennedy could only shake her head and laugh until tears welled in her eyes.

A second nurse approached the doorway and summoned, "Sharon Jeffries!" Amber and Kennedy stood on the other side of the door giggling quietly, and Reign took the bait, approaching the nurse and answering, "Yes, I'm Sharon."

Kennedy decided they would take the rapid test and wait, since the results only took twenty minutes, though it always felt like twenty-four hours when waiting for HIV results.

They sat silently watching TV in the lobby. After what seemed like an eternity, the first of the two nurses invited them back one by one for their results. Amber was first. The fifteen minutes it took for her to reemerge made Kennedy outrageously nervous. *Why would a negative result take so long to deliver?*

Finally, Amber came to the doorway smiling, and Kennedy was called back. As they passed each other, Amber whispered, "I'm fine, negative as usual." Kennedy followed the nurse into a small, fragrant room and took the only seat other than a desk chair. She wasn't the least bit worried, knowing she'd been celibate since her last negative test.

"Ms. Brown, I need to go over a few things with you."

"What are you trying to say?"

The nurse flashed a big smile, "Nothing, Ms. Brown, your results are negative."

"I was about to say," Kennedy spewed with an attitude, "you shouldn't play with people like that."

"I apologize, Ms. Brown; I didn't mean to scare you. I just figured you knew you were negative from your responses on the pre-test questionnaire. Celibacy usually indicates no change in HIV/AIDS status."

"I'm sorry. I guess my reaction proves this is a nerve-racking process for anyone."

"That's okay, Ms. Brown, I completely understand. Though I'd still like to talk with you about ways of maintaining your negative status." After finishing, Kennedy headed back to the waiting room. As she was walking up, the second nurse called Reign back.

"Ms. Jeffries?"

"Yes," Reign answered meekly.

"Is there an adult here with you today?"

"Yes, Ms. Kennedy and Ms. Amber."

"Who?" the nurse asked, confused.

"I mean..." Reign stumbled. "I meant to say Ms. Brown and Ms. Dixon."

"Okay, would you like them to come back with you?"

"Yes."

"Okay, Ms. Brown and Ms. Dixon, can you join us?" the nurse asked. The process felt different and somber for both Amber and Kennedy. They sensed something was wrong.

"Ladies, have a seat, please," the nurse offered, pointing to a row of three chairs in the office. She began, "Reign, how old are you?"

"Sixteen."

The nurse dropped her head for a millisecond, then stared into Reign's eyes and said, "Reign, your test came back positive for HIV."

Reign looked right through her without uttering a word. Beads of sweat began to form and spool down her forehead; her hands shook uncontrollably. Reign snapped out of her haze, only to glance over at Amber and Kennedy. Both were gazing at Reign in shock. Kennedy's chest tightened and her stomach began to bubble. She held Amber's hand as she wept.

Suddenly, Reign grabbed the edge of the chair, stood up and yelled to the top of her voice, "Noooo!" She fell to the floor in despair—completely inconsolable. "No, Lord, no! What did I do? No, no. It's not true. It can't be!" She looked up at the nurse and demanded, "Test me again, please! Do it again! Please, I've only been with one boy. It's not possible. Please, something's wrong with the test! It's gotta be the test! Please!"

Amber knelt down and held Reign as she rocked back and forth, continuing to beg the nurse to retest. "Reign, shhh, I got you, baby. It's going to be okay. I promise."

"No, Ms. Amber! I want her to test me again. Something's wrong with that test. I got the wrong results."

"Reign, I know it hurts. I know it hurts," Amber kept repeating. "Just let me help you, baby. You can get through this."

Abruptly, a manic calm appeared on Reign's face, "Ms. Amber, why me? I just wanted Todd to like me the way I liked him. I didn't mean to do anything wrong. I didn't even know I could hurt myself."

"I know, Reign. I know." Amber cried with a palpable ache while Kennedy sat frozen in her chair. Kennedy's only sign of life were the tears that rolled from her face and pounded her chest like a torrential rain.

The nurse did her best to comfort Reign with a long, gentle hug. Reign's head was hung as her agonizing sobs persisted.

"We need to contact Reign's parents or legal guardians," the nurse advised. Reign steadily moaned over the nurse's instructions. Amber kept rubbing her back, refusing to leave her side. "Once that's done, we'll be able to discuss next steps and refer Reign to a physician, if she doesn't already have one."

"That would be my mother," Reign choked out.

"I didn't understand," said the nurse.

"She said that would be her mother! You can call her mother!" Amber shouted.

"Reign, I know in the moment this means nothing to you, and probably won't bring much comfort, but with today's medical advances, an HIV-positive status is nothing like it was thirty years ago," the nurse vehemently encouraged, "This is a disease you can fight, Reign."

CHAPTER 19

Relax, Breathe, Push

"Ms. Kennedy! Ms. Kennedy!"

"Kayla, slow down. What's going on?"

"I can't! It's Ms. Alexis!"

"What about her?"

"I don't know; she breathing hard and she asked me to come get you."

"What?" As fast as her long legs would take her, Kennedy sprinted from behind her desk and hurried down a hallway and two flights of stairs. Kayla followed, struggling to keep up. When they reached her, Lexi she was bent over, holding her stomach. Kennedy could see the pain in her face. "Lexi, what's happening? Is it the baby?"

"It's ready to come; I think I'm in labor."

"What should we do, Ms. Kennedy?" Kayla asked uneasily.

"Yeah, Ms. Kennedy, how can we help?" Reign asked, appearing out of nowhere. "Kayla, run to my office. Grab my cell phone from my desk and my purse and keys from my closet. Reign, gather all of Lexi's personal stuff from her office. I'm taking her to my car. You two meet me there."

"Kennedy, I need you to call Ray!" Lexi yelled between taking deep breaths to control her contractions.

"I've got this, Lexi. I'll call him from the car. Right now, I need to get you to the hospital. Ain't no way in hell I can deliver this baby, and I damn sho don't want it to come in my car. My lease is almost up, and Auntie Kennedy don't want no mommy-baby juices all over her ride," Kennedy joked.

The closer they got to the hospital, the heavier Lexi's breathing became. She prayed, "Lord, help me," never ceasing with the breathing technique she'd learned in birthing class. Kennedy prayed, too, *Jesus, please don't let this baby drop out in my car; I don't want to have to torch the interior of my car. I love this car.*

When Lexi gave birth to her firstborn, Tré, it was a relatively predictable process. Lexi always tells the story about the day he was born. She checked into the hospital earlier that morning, and felt she needed to use the bathroom the entire afternoon. When the nurse finally checked Lexi, she could literally see the top of Tré's head. Her labor only lasted a couple of hours. It all happened so quickly, the baby popped out just as Ray arrived at the hospital.

Kennedy phoned Ray, Amber, and Reagan from the car and asked them to meet her at the hospital. This new baby was all of their bundle of joy. Everyone was so stoked, they could hardly wait.

Lexi, Kayla, Reign, and Kennedy arrived at St. Charity Hospital and pulled the car into the emergency room entrance. Kayla jumped out and announced to the whole triage station that Lexi was in labor. She could be heard all the way outside.

"My dance teacher is having a baby! Hey, lady, can you help us?"

"Calm down. Where is she?" a nurse inquired coolly.

"She's right outside in the car."

"Okay, we'll send somebody out with a wheelchair to get her."

"Send them now, please."

"Okay, let's get her inside so we can get them checked out," an attentive emergency room nurse said as he wheeled Lexi through double glass doors. At that instant, Lexi's water broke.

"Did she just pee on herself, Ms. Kennedy?" Kayla asked.

"No, baby, her water broke."

Several nurses scurried to get Lexi up to labor and delivery. Kennedy stayed at the registration desk and started filling out her admittance paperwork while the staff took care of Lexi. Kennedy knew most of the information and collected the missing pieces from Lexi's driver's license. Just as she was picking up her phone to call Ray again, he walked through the door.

"Where is she, Kennedy?" Ray asked frantically

"They just took her to labor and delivery."

"How's she doing?"

"Other than breathing like a moose, she appears to be doing well."

Ray waited until another nurse walked by and asked if could be escorted to Lexi's room.

Now, Reagan was calling, wanting to know where they were. "We're in labor and delivery at St. Charity Hospital," said Kennedy. "Where are you?"

"I just parked…about to walk in now. Were you able to reach Amber?"

"Yeah, she's on her way. Now let me get off the phone; you know I'm not supposed to have it on up here. We probably just stopped somebody's respirator!"

"Whatever! Bye, Kennedy."

Minutes later, like a perfectly choreographed commercial, Reagan arrived on one elevator as Amber exited the one right beside her.

"How did you two miss each other coming up?" Kennedy asked.

Flustered, Amber answered, "Because I went to the wrong floor. Some dumb lady at the front desk told me labor and delivery was on the fourth floor; I was in a whole 'nother wing of the hospital. How's Lexi and the baby?"

"Don't know yet."

"Where is she, Kennedy?"

"The nurses are trying to get her settled into her room."

"Is Ray here?" Reagan asked.

"He got here a few minutes ago."

"How is he?" asked Amber.

"A little rattled, as any expectant father would be," Kennedy answered.

"How did she get to the hospital?"

"I brought her. Kayla and Reign were in the studio with her when she started having contractions. Kayla came and alerted me, we all jumped in the car and brought her straight here."

"With her history of quick delivery, it's a good thing you were there," Amber said.

"Where are Kayla and Reign?" asked Reagan.

"Downstairs in the cafeteria. They should be back up in a minute. If Lexi hasn't delivered in a few hours, I'll run them home and come back. They were so thrilled to call their parents to tell them Lexi was having the baby. You would've thought they were getting a new sibling."

"How is Reign?" asked Amber.

"Today, she's doing okay," Kennedy answered, as Kayla and Reign walked off the elevator.

Amber directed the girls to take a spot on the couch directly across from them. The waiting area was luxurious, more like a hotel lobby. It had two large flat screen televisions and several cushy couches that were large enough to comfortably seat at least ten people.

"Kayla and Reign must have had enough to eat."

"How do you know, Kennedy?"

"Look at 'em. They are knocked out."

As the minutes dragged into hours, Kennedy's thoughts shifted to Reign. Watching her sleep brought tears to her eyes. The innocence of a child lost—with a single bad decision. She was such a young, energetic girl who wanted to do so much with her life. She had big dreams and hoped to achieve great things. Now the course would be altered by her HIV diagnosis.

A tap on the shoulder from Ray broke Kennedy's thoughts, "Hey, I just came out to let you guys know Lexi just started pushing. Kennedy, the doctor said you can come in now."

"I want to go, too!" said Amber and Reagan simultaneously.

"I don't think that'll be a problem. Let me go ask," said Ray.

Kennedy looked back at Reign again and felt overwhelmed by all she'd had to endure. She wanted to snatch her up, hug her, and never let go. Instead, she gently leaned in, told her she loved her, and shared she was going back to see Lexi.

Groggily awakening from her sleep, Reign asked, "Did she have the baby yet?"

"Not yet, but it'll be here shortly." As she sat up on the couch, Kennedy put her arms around Reign and fought back tears that put a lump in her throat. *If only I could have protected her.*

A minute later, Ray came out again and yelled for everyone to hurry. Kennedy was a ball of nerves. She covered the gamut of emotions: tearful, overjoyed, anxious, afraid. Not to mention the anticipation of learning the baby's sex—Lexi and Ray had wanted to be surprised. Kennedy couldn't stop crying. Amber was Tré's godmother, so it was only fitting that Kennedy would hold the title for Lexi's second child. Watching Lexi bring her first godchild into the world multiplied Kennedy's angst. *How am I going to protect this child from this crazy world?*

"Ladies, I'm going to ask you to stand over here so we'll have room to maneuver once the baby comes out," a nurse named Diane asked politely. Lexi was impressively calm. *I hope I can be that calm during childbirth,* Kennedy wished.

Lexi held to her breathing protocol and reciting the twenty-third Psalm. It was her own form of meditation and relaxation, and it seemed to work well. She wasn't ranting and raving, screaming at the doctor to get that "thing" out of her, or faulting Ray for putting her in such a predicament. She just laid there panting, breathing, and praying.

Dr. Cunningham entered the room for his final check and announced to Nurse Diane, "I think it's time." Then he looked at Lexi and asked, "Okay, Alexis, ready to have your baby?"

Other than pain, it was the first visible sign of emotion from Lexi as she grabbed her stomach and confessed, "I'm as ready as I'll ever be." She took several deep, grunting breaths. Diane instructed Ray to bend one of Alexis' knees close to her body, while she did the same with the other.

"Alexis, I need you to breathe just like you've been doing, except this time when I say push, take a big, deep breath, exhale, and push again."

"I'll try, Diane."

"Push, Alexis."

Lexi took a deep breath, exhaled, and pushed.

Diane encouraged Lexi, "Good job, now breathe in and out, in and out. Keep pushing."

Lexi took another deep breath, exhaled, and pushed. Dr. Cunningham finally spoke. "Alexis, I see the baby's head. Ray, don't be afraid to take a look." Kennedy's waterworks show started back up as she, too, could see her godchild's head. *What kind of godmother will I be? Will the baby be able to talk to me about anything? If only Reign had a godmother she could've talked to. How do you make children comfortable enough to talk to you about anything?* Kennedy found it impossible to focus and clear her racing thoughts.

"One more time, Alexis, push!" Dr. Cunningham ordered.

Lexi inhaled, exhaled, and pushed. This time, she didn't stop pushing.

"That's it, Alexis. Keep on pushing. Keep pushing." Kennedy wondered if Dr. Cunningham got excited with each baby she delivered. She couldn't see how she managed to handle the emotion of it all. How did she stay sane and keep from becoming a basket case in the delivery room?

Diane and Dr. Cunningham both urged, "Almost there, Alexis. Keep pushing." Dr. Cunningham reached her hands around the baby's head and back, pulling it out, and just like that, another life had peeped into the world—a baby girl.

As the doctor placed her on Lexi's chest, there wasn't a dry eye in the delivery room. "Aww, it's a girl. A baby girl!" Lexi cried out. Kennedy really lost it then. She was soaking wet from her eyes down to the top of her t-shirt.

"Kennedy, come see your godchild," Ray said.

"She's beautiful," was all Kennedy managed to get out.

Diane asked everyone to leave and allow the team to get Lexi and the baby taken care of. Back in the waiting room, Reign shouted, "Ms. Kennedy, what did she have?"

"It's a baby girl."

"How much does she weigh? Did she name her?"

"Not yet, Kayla. They're doing all of that now."

"How is Ms. Lexi?"

"She's doing fine, Reign."

Kennedy just couldn't resist wrapping her arms around Reign one more time and giving her the biggest hug ever.

"How are you doing, sweetheart?" she asked Reign.

"I'm okay, Ms. Kennedy."

"Reign, you are so special to me. I want you to know I'm going to be with you every step of the way, through this whole thing. It's going to be very important for you to listen to your doctors and do exactly as they tell you, okay?"

"I will, Ms. Kennedy, I promise."

Reign started to cry, and she squeezed Kennedy like never before. Kennedy held her embrace and assured her she still had so much living to do. "God has a plan for you, baby. Stay strong and hold on," she told Reign. Their tears kept coming, and Kennedy hated herself for not having the power to do anything to make it better. *She's just a child; she doesn't deserve this harsh penalty for her naive mistake.* No matter what, Kennedy knew she had to support Reign and stick by her side.

Ray entered the waiting room with wonderful news that shifted the energy. "Hey, everybody, the baby weighs eight pounds and five ounces, and she's nineteen inches long."

"What's her name?" Amber yelled.

"We named her A'dra Reign."

Reign looked up from Kennedy's bosom and wiped the tears from her face, asking, "Mr. Roberts, you all gave her my name?"

"Yes, Reign, we thought it was only fitting since after the Reign, there is always sunshine. Keep your head up, baby girl. We are all here to see you through this."

"Thank you, Mr. Roberts. Will you kiss Ms. Alexis and Baby Reign for me? Ms. Kennedy, can you believe it? They named her after me!"

"I heard, Reign. That's amazing. Why don't we all go to the nursery and see Baby A'dra Reign?"

As the whole crew approached the window of the nursery, it was clear all had baby fever. Even Reagan was ready to have a baby of her own;

with her and Ryan making plans to start their family. Amber crooned over how plump A'dra was. She was a big baby, especially for a woman as little as Lexi. Kennedy studied A'dra through the nursery window. She wondered again, *how will I shield you from all the deadly evils of this world? I couldn't protect Reign; she was just an innocent child looking for love, now she's HIV-positive. How will I save you?*

CHAPTER 20

Just One More Thing Before "I Do"

Walking through the front doors of the church, Kennedy could feel the love and serenity fueling her wedding day. It would be the day Orray Philips would make her Kennedy Johnson-Phillips. Guests were starting to arrive, with bellowing excitement and jovial voices of the bridal party echoing in the church corridors.

Fragrant florals throughout the venue awakened every sense. Colorful lilies and simple carnations accented with baby's breath flooded the church foyer. The sanctuary was adorned with roses of every color and kind: red and white garden roses, yellow, pink, and orange miniature roses, and the altar was dressed with hundreds of fully bloomed red cottage, tiffany, and modern roses.

Every pew was capped with huge satin damask bows. Six-foot stainless steel Swarovski-draped candelabras framed the left and right side of the altar, each holding twenty 11-inch crimson and crème taper candles. It was the magnificent, fairytale setting Kennedy had always envisioned.

Moses had instructed the bridal party to arrive at the church two hours before the ceremony. He was bound and determined to ensure no one's last-minute arrival would delay the start of the wedding, especially the bride and groom. There were more participants in the wedding than on an NBA team, but pomp and circumstance was par for the course for a professional player's wedding.

Kennedy and Orray were able to successfully manage keeping the media away. In fact, only a handful of media persons were invited. Kennedy also hired her Cleveland Police friends to patrol the church's perimeter and prevent the entry of any uninvited guests.

Kayla and Reign were junior bridesmaids while Amber, Lexi, and Reagan served as bridesmaids. To reduce stress and avoid picking a favorite, Kennedy opted not to have a maid of honor, though her first choice would have been Lexi. She had gone through so much with each woman, and considered all her attendants deserving of honor. While the title of maid was more befitting for Amber, since she could always be found cleaning up one of her disastrous relationship.

All the ladies had arrived impressively on time and all had settled into the bridal dressing room to start hair and makeup. Lexi was the last to arrive and made her way straight to Kennedy, even before hanging up her dress. "Congratulation, sweetheart! I couldn't be happier for you. You're more worthy of this day than anyone I know."

"Lexi. Thank you so much. Don't make me cry," Kennedy gushed.

"Oh, please don't, Ken. I need to run and get started on my makeup, but I wanted us to have a quick chat first. Do you mind?"

"Sure, talk to me."

"Well, I know my timing sucks and this is probably the last thing you want to talk about on your wedding day, but I wouldn't be able to sleep tonight if I didn't ask you something. Did you have the you-know-what talk with Orray yet?

"You-know-what?"

"Kennedy, don't play dumb with me. You can't keep this from that man."

"Honest to God, Lexi. I just don't know how to do it." Kennedy was already on edge with wedding jitters, and Lexi bringing up the topic was enough to tip the scale. She was infuriated and began to yell at Lexi,

"How do I do it, Lexi? Huh? Should I just blurt it out? Hey, Orray. Guess what? I slept with Rick—you know, the guy you kick it with every weekend; your good friend from college. Your freggin teammate! Know who I'm talking about? Yeah, Rick, that's who! Just thought you should know I slept with your boy!"

With a look of repulsion on her face, Lexi lashed back. "I don't know if that's how you should tell him, but yeah, that's exactly what you need to tell him! Look, Kennedy, Orray's the professional gamer in the relationship, not you! It's time out for your games. You have got to tell him, and you've gotta go out there and do it now!"

"It's my wedding day, Lexi. I can't! I might lose everything!"

"Kennedy, you might lose everything if you don't! Please, don't start your marriage on a path of deception."

Kennedy walked away from Lexi to take a second to mentally recover. She hated the thought of crying before her ceremony or having her makeup run down her face like a circus clown. It had taken an hour to apply and was still only partially done. So she fought back the tears and coached herself through the moment. *Do I take this secret to my grave, or take the risk of admitting to Orray that Rick and I were once lovers?*

It was a mental and physical pressure that weighed on her like a two-ton elephant. But Alexis was right; she had to tell him. She couldn't allow another minute to pass without having the conversation. Her brain vacillated. *What if he leaves me at the altar? But, if I don't tell him, there'll always be this dark cloud over my head. Lord, help me, please.*

After the birth of her godchild, Kennedy had sworn she was all cried out and didn't have any tears left. *This is my day. I'm getting married, finally. I'm not going to ruin it or allow anyone else to. My destiny is based on my decisions. I have to do what's best for me. But what about Orray? He has a right to know. What man could deal with the realization that his wife and his boy had been together? He won't be able to handle it.*

No amount of wavering could justify keeping Orray in the dark, and everything holy in Kennedy screamed she had to tell him. There was no difference in a half-truth and a lie. Lexi had spoken the truth. Kennedy knew she'd be doomed going into her marriage with secrets.

"Can someone get Orray for me?" she quietly asked, with her head buried in her chest.

Moses came running out of nowhere. "Kennedy, what are you doing, chil'? The groom should never see his bride before the wedding."

"I know, Moses, but this is urgent. I need to talk to him, somewhere privately. Lexi, call his cell phone and tell him to meet me downstairs."

Kennedy also believed in the tradition of the bride and groom not seeing each other before the ceremony, but in the bigger scheme of things, it was just a dumb tradition. Besides, she hadn't completed her makeup or put on her gown yet. If he decided to go on with the wedding, Orray wouldn't have the slightest idea of how she'd look fully made up and dressed. Though, there was a lingering chance there wouldn't be a need for a final look, or a donning of her $4,000 Vera Wang wedding gown. She could already see the next day's newspaper headline: "Orray Phillips Dumps Untrustworthy Bride at Altar."

"I got him. He's waiting for you near the sanctuary, Kennedy," Lexi said, giving her a tender hug. "You're doing the right thing, babe. You'll feel so much better afterwards."

"Let's hope so," Kennedy mumbled somberly. The walk to the first floor was the longest of her life. Special moments of her relationship with Orray played like a streaming movie in her mind. She knew the memories would be permanently embedded and all that was left of Orray, if he walked away.

"Orray, where are you?"

"I'm in here, baby." Orray had taken a seat in a small prayer room right off the sanctuary. "Honey, what is it?" He jumped to his feet and walked toward Kennedy as she entered the room. "Why did you need to see me so suddenly? Baby, please don't tell me you're having second thoughts."

"About marrying you? Never. You're the best thing that's ever happened to me, Orray. I know you'll find this hard to believe, but I imagined this day the first time I laid eyes on you, down to the crimson and crème candles out there in the sanctuary. And here we are now, living out that daydream. You should know I've never had a second thought about doing anything with you."

"Then what's wrong?"

Kennedy could feel her legs turning into jelly; she staggered toward a nearby bench to sit. Taking a deep breath she began, "Actually, when it's all said and done, I think you might be the one who'll have second thoughts."

"Why would I second guess making you my wife?"

"The fear that's crawling all over me right now is real, but at the same time, I know confessing a big secret on our wedding day may sound like some corny B-movie."

"Babe, you killin' me. Come on. Spit it out. What's so important it couldn't wait until after you become Mrs. Philips?"

"I...umm...I..." Kennedy stalled to catch her breath again. "Orray, I...I never told you the truth about my relationship with Rick, but we're umm....we're more than play sister and brother. Baby, Rick and I used to be lovers. He was actually the last guy I slept with before practicing celibacy." She paused to gauge Orray's reaction.

Orray was quiet for a moment, but it felt like hours to Kennedy. Then his silence was broken by an illuminating smile that hijacked his face. "I can't believe this, Kennedy," was all he managed to say.

Is this his way of dealing with severe disappointment? Kennedy wondered. Was he suppressing cussing her out with a big, nervous smile?

"Kennedy, I can't believe this."

"Orray, it's the truth."

"No, I can't believe this is what you called me downstairs to talk about. Kennedy, I know about you and Rick."

"You do?"

"Yeah, come on. Guys talk, just like women. Rick told me the first night I asked about you. He told me he'd had an intimate relationship with you a few years back, but the intimacy turned into a friendship once you guys broke up."

"You're not upset about it?"

"How can I be?"

"Because, I never told you, Orray."

"Kennedy, just because you don't tell me something, doesn't mean I can't find it out. Now, don't get me wrong, I think you should've come clean sooner. I didn't think it would take you this long. Truthfully, I really don't care about your past; all I care about is your future, with me. We all have spots in our past that didn't come out in the wash. Sin sometimes puts us in situations that interrupt God's plan for our lives. And when we make decisions outside of his will, we get tossed into stuff that can be detrimental, but he always forgives and redirects us. Rick never labeled you as a groupie or some fly-by-night hoochie. He made it a point to tell me that you were someone he really cared about. He just wasn't ready for the type of commitment you needed. He even told me that if I didn't do right by you, he'd kill me."

"Oh my God, I'm sweating like a pig. I'm so relieved, baby. I thought you would never forgive me. Orray, how could I not love you?"

"It's the past, Kennedy. I just want to marry you, and I want to do it today. But before you get dolled up to walk down that aisle, you gotta promise me you'll always tell me when something's bothering you, no matter how small it seems. Please don't let me be the last to know."

"I will. I'll tell you. I promise."

"Okay, now can we do the real I will and I do's?"

"Yes, my love. Absolutely! Will you meet me back here in an hour?" Kennedy asked.

"Wouldn't wanna be any other place on the planet. Now go put on that dress," Orray ordered, slapping her on the booty.

Kennedy rushed back to her dressing room to finish getting powdered, primped, outfitted, and tousled. She marveled over the stature of the man God had blessed her with. He was a forgiving soul who refused to waste time on things that were out of his control. He was a model human being for celebrating life and living in the present.

"How'd it go?" Lexi asked, rushing over to Kennedy while simultaneously taking down the pinned curls from her hair.

"Lexi, he already knew."

"Let me guess, blabbermouth Rick."

"You know it. He said Rick gave him the 4-1-1 that first night I saw him at Ruby's."

"Thank the Lord Orray is a mature man! I prayed the whole time you were downstairs. But, after you were gone for fifteen minutes, I started going through ways we could flip the wedding reception into a Liberation Party. Girl, I had already put together my George W. Bush speech, asking guests to allow you to keep their wedding gifts as a consolation prize for being kicked to the curb."

"Lexi, I can always count on your shameless comedic relief," Kennedy smiled.

"You know I'm always in your corner, gurl. I'm so proud of you! I knew it would turn out just the way it did, and now the best is yet to come. Ready to polish off the old and bring in the new?"

"Are you kidding me? Yes! Now, go finish getting dressed, Lexi. Let's get this show on the road!" Kennedy said, whipping her head around the room to see the progress of the rest of the girls. "Hey, has anyone seen my veil?" she yelled, instantly switching into Operation Bridezilla Mode.

"Over here, Kennedy. I'll help you with it as soon as your makeup's finished."

"Thanks, Reagan."

The final touches were all about perfecting Kennedy's makeup, putting on sexy undergarments, and the piece de résistance—her Vera Wang gown. It was a champagne-colored silk and lace creation that took six months to make. The strapless sweetheart neckline showed off Kennedy's toned arms and back, and the chandelier beaded bodice flaunted her trim waistline. The twenty-foot train was constructed from Italian lace with a collective seventy hours of hand beading. When she was all dressed and lavished in the exquisite four-carat teardrop diamond necklace and matching earrings Orray had sent over the evening before, Regan placed her veil on her head. She did it with the precision of a professional, and Kennedy knew Reagan's every placement and tuck was shrouded in love.

"You look unbelievable," Amber said, stepping backwards to take in Kennedy's whole look.

"Thanks, Amber."

"Okay, honey. This is it. You ready?"

"Yes, Lexi. I can't believe I'm saying this, but yes, I'm ready to get married."

As Kennedy made it downstairs to the closed sanctuary doors, she could hear the melodic sounds of the harpist playing. All the bridesmaids had taken their turns, individually strutting down the 30-foot hand-painted aisle. Now, it was Kennedy's moment.

She approached the beautiful, mahogany double doors of the century-old chapel. It felt like a castle, and she was the queen going to meet her king. The heavy doors swinging open was Kennedy's cue to begin her walk down the aisle. She and her father entered the church, walking arm in arm to the sweet sounds of *Love* by Kirk Franklin. She held her daddy tightly, trying to remember to put her left foot in front of the right, but her nervous feet had a brain of their own and decided on something different. It felt like she had two left feet in casts.

Her mother was nestled prominently in the first row, weeping tears of joy, and Kennedy's grandparents were seated nearby, adding more delight to the atmosphere. Halfway into their walk down the aisle, her father whispered, "This is your day, baby girl, and you look as beautiful as your mother did on our wedding day 37 years ago." His words immediately put tears in Kennedy's eyes. She had held back for as long as she could.

Hearing all the sniffles from their guests, it was clear that Kennedy and Orray's friends and family were also moved by the day. Looking down the end of the aisle, Kennedy laid eyes on Orray for the first time in his wedding attire. The coco-chocolate man from the gym was dressed in a black tux—positioned front and center at the altar. His broad shoulders and muscles perfectly contoured every seam of his jacket. His hair was freshly cut; his beard and mustache highlighted the richness of his skin. He was exactly as she saw him in her head the day in the gym when she'd fantasized about him becoming her husband.

Pastor Williams began, "Dearly beloved, we are gathered here today in the presence of God and these witnesses, to join Kennedy Marie Johnson and Orray Eugene Phillips in holy matrimony."

And in what seemed like an instant, it was time for Kennedy's vows: "Orray, I have waited a lifetime for you. When I asked God to send me a husband, I never knew he would send me a gift wrapped in a package of godliness, fidelity, and forgiveness. So today, you are the proof that my prayers have been answered. With this ring, I promise to love, cherish, and respect you for the rest of my days, till death do us part."

Orray followed: "Kennedy, you are my gift and blessing from God. Not once did I ever doubt that you were the woman for me. You live with such dignity and a sense of service to others that my love has grown for you daily. Having you in my life has made it fuller, richer, and deeply spiritual. Now, today, I gladly make you my wife. With this ring I place on your finger, it is my promise to love, cherish, honor, and respect you till death do us part. I love you."

After Orray and Kennedy's vows, Pastor Williams challenged, "Into this holy estate these two people present now come to be joined. If any persons can show just cause why they should not be joined together, let them speak now or forever hold their peace." Kennedy stood still, squeezing her eyes tightly, hoping only to hear silence. The next voice she heard was the welcoming baritone of Pastor Williams. "Well then, by the power vested in me by the state of Ohio, I pronounce you husband and wife. You may kiss your bride!" Pastor Williams declared, giving a nod to Orray.

"Boooy, I can't wait until tonight, Mrs. Philips," Orray said, leaning in to Kennedy and planting a big, wet kiss between her crimson red-stained lips.

"Oh God, me neither. Can we go now?" Kennedy teased.

Breaking their long, wet kiss with his ceremonious announcement, the pastor shouted, "Ladies and gentlemen, I present to you Mr. and Mrs. Orray Eugene Phillips!" Kennedy and Orray turned and faced a standing room only sanctuary of guests. Stevie Wonder's "Signed, Sealed, Delivered I'm Yours" blared though the speakers as the wedding party formed to exit the chapel. Spontaneously, the entire congregation stood, clapping with thundering applause, as dozens of hands reached out to touch and congratulate the newly joined couple.

Kennedy and Orray were quickly whisked off in a vintage Rolls Royce to their chic downtown reception at the Ritz Carlton. They'd secured the two largest rooms and combined them to create one stunning gala. Each chair and table was draped in organza silk and accented with a magnificent 100-count assorted rose centerpiece. Every guest's name was engraved in a stainless steel table tent and placed in front of a crimson and crème china place setting.

Kennedy and Orray entered the reception hand in hand, going straight to the dance floor, and having their first dance to "At Last" by Ella Fitzgerald. There were nearly 400 friends and family members in attendance. Guests were treated to a full bar of premium liquors and imported champagne. The couple had spared no expense in their selection of hand-passed hors d'oeuvres: oysters on the half shell, lamb kabobs, shrimp cocktail, and duck pâté on water crackers. The sit-down dinner was no less impressive, beginning with a salad of mixed greens, organic cherry tomatoes, fresh-baked garlic croutons, and a balsamic bourbon dressing. The main course was filet mignon, lobster tails, asparagus, and smoked Gouda potatoes au gratin. Their five-tier wedding cake was a yellow, butter cream, decadent monstrosity, and the groom's red velvet cake was featured on its own table. It was designed and fully decorated to simulate a live NBA game. No details were omitted, as the designer masterfully used fondant to construct a court, players, coaches, bleachers, fans, and all things basketball. It was truly a work of art.

Orray, Kennedy, and their guests danced like the night would never end. Though the wedding and every particular regarding it was extravagant, the dancing got pretty ghetto. Kennedy had ordered the deejay not to play a single line dance song, but seeing the way their guests packed the floor for the biker shuffle and wobble, she was embarrassed she'd ever made such a frivolous request. After all, she had more important things to place her attention on, like saving every dance for Orray.

"I didn't know you could move like that, Mr. Phillips," she flirted with her new husband.

"Of course you didn't! I couldn't show you everything in my arsenal until you became my wife," Orray shot back.

"Lucky me," Kennedy said, covering Orray's face with loving kisses.

"Congratulations, guys," a voice sounded off behind them. They both turned to see Rick standing there, dressed neatly in a navy blue suit and coordinating bowtie.

"Thanks, man," said Orray.

"Yeah, we appreciate you being responsible for our meeting. I may have missed out on the man of my dreams had you not told him who I was that night at Ruby's," Kennedy said.

"Hey, no biggie. I was happy to tell him how terrific of a woman you are."

"I'm truly grateful Rick." Kennedy certainly wanted to have more words with Rick; some only had four letters, but her bits of anger were short-lived. She had come clean about their relationship, Orray hadn't waivered in his love, and their wedding was her dream come true. She had no reason to hold onto or rehash anything with Rick. He was officially a buried part of her past.

The night continued, and the ambiance became more romantic as the sun set and the reception was only lit by the moon and candlelight. The guests had been royally fed and a couple hundred bottles of champagne served. Not a soul left the night feeling less than spoiled.

Kennedy was reminded of how nightfall was the universal signal for all minors to go home, as Kayla and Reign approached her with long faces. "Ms. Kennedy, my mama said it's time for us to go," Reign pouted.

"Oh, don't look so sad, girls," Kennedy encouraged. "You both looked so pretty today. Did you have a good time?"

"Yeees!" they said in unison.

"Good, I'm glad you got to be a part of today. Seeing you girls at the altar made me smile."

"Oh! Ms. Kennedy, guess what?" Reign shouted as if she had almost forgotten something.

"What, hon?

"I saw my doctor this week and he started me on my medicine. He said if I'm serious about taking my meds and following his orders, I could basically live a normal life. I may even be able to get married one day, like you, Ms. Kennedy."

"Reign, that's the second-best news I've heard all day. Congratulations, baby. I told you. See, there is sunshine after Reign."

"Yep. Hey, you said mine was the second-best news you heard today. What was the first?"

"Well, when Pastor Williams announced Orray and me husband and wife, of course."

"Duh, what'd you think, Reign?" Kayla taunted.

"Girls, come on. We gotta go!" Reign's mother yelled from the distance.

"Okay, we 'bout to get in trouble, Ms. Kennedy," Kayla said, hugging Kennedy hurriedly.

"All right, girls, you be safe. I love you both to pieces. Bye!"

"Byyye," they sang like a song, hurrying off to catch up with Reign's mom.

Suddenly the deejay gave an order for the dance floor to clear and Reagan appeared, setting a chair in the middle of the floor. Grabbing Kennedy's hand, she led her to the chair to sit. Most of Kennedy's sands had followed her dating trials and were anxious to give her a sorority serenade. As her sorority sisters joined hands, they encircled her and began to sing. Reagan locked eyes with Kennedy and mouthed the words, "I love you." Kennedy responded with a wink and a stream of tears.

"Kennedy, I can't even find the words to express how delighted I am for you," Reagan shared at the end of the song.

"You don't have to. I already know. Thank you, Reagan," Kennedy said, squeezing her in a hug as tightly as she could.

"Well, all of this love has made me want to make some of my own. I think I'm gonna find my Ray and we're going upstairs to our room for a lil sumthin-sumthin."

"Girl, I hear ya, same here," Alexis said, approaching the two.

"Hey, girlie! Where's my godbaby?" Kennedy asked Alexis.

"My mother-in-law took her home. She was cranky, and it was well past her bedtime."

"Awww, I wanted some sugar before she left," said Kennedy.

"Sorry. Look, Kennedy, just wanted to let you know Amber is over at the bar talking 'bout she leaving with some man. I don't even have the energy to chaperone her foolishness tonight. I'm completely exhausted, so I think I'm going to take it in, too."

"Okay, Lexie. Thank you and Reagan so much for all your help, with everything."

"Kennedy, my friend, go in peace and love! You are a blessed woman. Today, you married your match."

"I did indeed! I appreciate you so much, Lexi. Love you to death."

"I love you too, pal. Now, let me make a mad dash, before Amber comes over here with all her lunacy." Hugging Lexi goodnight, Kennedy could see Amber approaching over her shoulder. "Just remember," Alexis cautioned, "No head spins tonight. Take it easy on Orray."

"Girl! Go! Bye." Kennedy chuckled uncontrollably, knowing that Lexi's warning was much needed. She was ready for some serious bedroom action with her new hubby.

"Kennedy, girl, you better werk that Orray over tonight! Don't have that man regretting he married you before testing the waters. None of that trying to be humble stuff. You betta be down with the A-game tonight, huntey!" Amber schooled Kennedy.

"Okay, playgirl," Kennedy laughed.

"Speaking of testing the waters, I'm heading out with that cutie in the purple shirt over at the bar. He's been at me all night, and his NBA status aside, I feel like we may have some real chemistry."

"Girl, do you ever go anywhere without meeting a man?"

"Hmmm, not usually! An-tee-way, I'm out! Love you, Ken-Ken. Remember, don't give Orray reason for regret!"

"I thought you were leaving, Amber? Bye!" Kennedy poked.

Turning to hunt for Orray, Kennedy didn't realize he was just a couple of steps away. He swiftly reached for her. Doubling his long arms around every inch of her waist he propositioned, "So, Mrs. Philips, would you like to join your husband upstairs in the honeymoon suite?"

"I thought you'd never ask!"

Like two teenagers in heat, they raced through the hallways leading to the elevators. The whole reception they'd anticipated going to their room and finally making love. *I can now make love to my husband,* she thought. It was a sacred moment of closeness she'd longed for; now the moment had come she could give herself to her husband.

Behind the doors of their suite, Orray unzipped her gown to reveal her silk corset, stockings, and garter belt. His large hands felt warm and supple on her back. He caressed her shoulders and neck like he was experiencing touching her for the first time. He kissed her face, her shoulders, her breasts, and her stomach—no parts of her were off limits.

Kennedy began to cry.

"Baby, why are you crying?" Orray asked.

"Because, it just hit me that for the first time in my life, I know what it feels like to be truly loved. What I'm feeling with you now is something I've never felt before."

"Just wait, there's more," Orray said sensually.

Kennedy could smell his skin and feel the heat coming from his mouth. It was a titillating combination that made her quiver in pleasure. She threw both hands over her head in surrender and Orray laced his ten fingers into hers. For a still second, the room was quiet, followed by gratifying moans from both.

They had become one.

Made in the USA
Lexington, KY
16 April 2019